Vermont ICONS

Vermont ICONS

50 CLASSIC SYMBOLS OF
THE GREEN MOUNTAIN STATE

Jennifer Smith-Mayo
and Matthew P. Mayo

Guilford, Connecticut

Photos by Jennifer Smith-Mayo, except where otherwise noted.
Text by Matthew P. Mayo.

Project editor: Meredith Dias
Text design/layout: Casey Shain

Library of Congress Cataloging-in-Publication Data
Mayo, Matthew P.
      Vermont icons : 50 classic symbols of the Green Mountain State /
Jennifer Smith-Mayo and Matthew P. Mayo.
          p. cm.
      "Photos by Jennifer Smith-Mayo"—T.p. verso.
      Includes bibliographical references and index.
        ISBN 978-0-7627-7145-5 (alk. paper)
      1. Historic sites—Vermont. 2. Vermont—Social life and customs. 3.
Vermont—History—20th century. 4. Historic sites—Vermont—Pictorial
works. 5. Vermont—Social life and customs—Pictorial works. 6.
Vermont—History—Pictorial works. I. Smith-Mayo, Jennifer. II. Title.
        F49.M39 2012
        974.3—dc23
                                                            2011048050

Printed in the United States of America
10 9 8 7 6 5 4 3 2 1

*To Francis John Smith, whose kindness
and great love of Vermont endures in us all.*

CONTENTS

INTRODUCTION

One of many happy coincidences the two of us share in life is that when we were youngsters, our parents chose to relocate their families to northern Vermont's fabled Northeast Kingdom—inspired decisions for which we remain grateful. While there is nothing wrong with where we came from (Ohio in Jen's case, Rhode Island in Matt's), as anyone who has spent time in the Green Mountain State will tell you, there is something singular and magical about Vermont.

Not only did our families move to her green hills, they put down roots here. Matt's parents continued the family trade of dairy farming on the banks of the Missisquoi River in Westfield, while Jen's parents owned a general store in scenic Irasburg. Though in many ways idealized, these bucolic ways of life nonetheless helped make our formative years largely idyllic, and Vermont's lush and alluring great outdoors changed us in ways we're thankful for to this day. We fished, hunted, skied, skated, sledded, hiked, biked, snowmobiled, and camped, and we have yet to tire of Vermont's natural offerings. We also helped to make maple syrup; fetched cows in from the pasture; lent a hand with haying; cut, split, and stacked firewood (then hauled it into the house to burn and carried the ashes out again); shared early morning coffee with town carpenters, plumbers, and dump-truck drivers; and so much more.

Given our long personal histories with and abiding love for the Green Mountain State, we set about the daunting task of sugaring down to fifty the essential elements that best represent this vast, rich region. The book offers plenty of expected (for good reason) people, places, events, and products that help make Vermont her unique self, among them general stores, covered bridges, cows, Ben & Jerry's ice cream, and maple syrup. But we also hope you will be surprised and pleased by other less obvious inclusions, such as back roads, *no* billboards, woodpiles, Bag Balm, and mud season.

Because Vermont is brimming with iconic elements, we were left with a long list of noteworthies that you won't find in these pages, such as the New England Culinary Institute, Vergennes (Vermont's smallest and oldest city), Basketville, King Arthur Flour Company, farm stands, Vermont Yankee Nuclear Power Plant, witch windows (those sideways panes peculiar to Vermont), and the long, colorful tradition of quilting in the Green Mountains.

And how about all those fascinating facts we didn't have room for: That in 1864, St. Albans was the site of the northernmost skirmish of the Civil War? Or that in 1846, the Brattleboro postmaster licked the US government in the race to issue postage stamps—by a full year? Or that public nudity is not illegal in Vermont (though disrobing in public is), which might explain why World Naked Bike Ride has been such a popular festivity in the Green Mountain State? And how about ethnic diversity? Not so much, as it turns out: Vermont is one of the "whitest" states in the United States, surpassed only by its near neighbor, Maine. And why do so many socially responsible companies start up and continue to operate in the state that cradled them in their infancy? Perhaps there is, indeed, something in the water.

Though we now reside in Maine, our families still live in Vermont and we visit them frequently throughout the year. Each time we wind through the curving roads deep in the heart of the Green Mountain's majesty to get back home again (for Vermont is as much our home as anywhere can be), no matter the season (be it winter, spring, mud, summer, or autumn), we always comment that we're pleased there's still no direct east–west route from Maine through New Hampshire to Vermont. Think of all those lovely little river and mountain towns that would be bypassed in favor of speed.

We encourage people to veer off the soulless paved highways and venture wherever their exploring hearts take them. Vermont's rolling green hills and lush colorful valleys, her snowy peaks and rushing rivers, her quiet villages and nod-and-wave people all have a bewitching effect on anyone lucky enough to find themselves rambling her byways. We count ourselves fortunate to be among those roving explorers. Perhaps we'll see you out there, too.

Cheers,
The Mayos

P.S. As fond as we are of Vermont, rarely has one's love of a place been as heartfelt or stated more eloquently as when thirtieth US President Calvin Coolidge spoke of his home state on September 21, 1928:

Vermont is a state I love. I could not look upon the peaks of Ascutney, Killington, Mansfield, and Equinox without being moved in a way that no other scene could move me. It was here that I first saw the light of day; here I received my bride; here my dead lie pillowed on the loving breast of our everlasting hills. I love Vermont because of her hills and valleys, her scenery and invigorating climate, but most of all, because of her indomitable people. They are a race of pioneers who have almost beggared themselves to serve others. If the spirit of liberty should vanish from other parts of the union and support of our institutions should languish, it could all be replenished from the generous store held by the people of this brave little state of Vermont.

VERMONT ICONS

VERMONTERS

When confronted with an eager, young out-of-stater who said he was pleased to meet him, an old Vermont bachelor farmer said, "You don't know that yet." Then he winked.

The honeyed tongue of the old-time, native Vermonter is famous, as much for what is left unsaid as for what is said.

Should a Vermonter welcome you into his hearth and home, he may well offer you a medley of tasty fare: red-flannel hash, venison stew, maple sinkers (donuts), dilly beans, and apple pie. Enjoy! But you might want to gird yourself for a little ribbing, especially if you're a "flatlander," which in a Vermonter's purview means anyone from anywhere that isn't Vermont. Rocky Mountains be damned!

Vermonters are widely regarded as independent minded, thumbing their noses at anyone who dares to tell them what to think, how to vote, when to plant their gardens, or why a newfangled gadget will help them can beets safer or split wood faster. Yet, they like to socialize, too, as evidenced in the preponderance throughout the state of public suppers, town hall dances, and early-

For more information about Vermont and her proud people: www.vermont vacation.com

morning general-store chin wags around the coffee pot.

Vermonters are big on family events, too, many of which take place outdoors. Ice fishing and snowmobiling top the list in the colder months (all eight of them), while the warmer weather finds town commons filled with baseball teams and ponds and lakes hosting numerous boats bristling with rods. When they're not playing hard, Vermonters are working hard, making do with several side jobs, plus gardening and filling the freezer—which, along with an ample woodpile, is a Vermonter's surest insurance policy.

Vermontese is a measured northern drawl as inscrutable at times as it is enchanting. Where else are you likely to be called "mister bubby," regardless of your gender? Or hear the phrase "Jeezum Crowby!" as an exclamation of surprise? Or "couple three" instead of "two or three"? Should you appear not to be working hard enough at a task, you may be told to "come onto it." And yes, in Vermont you really will hear the word "Ayuh" as a term of assessment and agreement.

NO BILLBOARDS

One of the lovely things about getting out and about in the Green Mountain State is that you can actually see the Green Mountains. From the top to the bottom of the state, you won't find a billboard lining Vermont's highways and byways. That is thanks, in large part, to one man: Theodore M. Riehle Jr., a Navy officer, veteran of three wars, and nonnative of Vermont who fell passionately in love with her natural charms. He despaired of seeing her become littered with "unregulated outdoor advertising," the visual clutter that at the time was popping up along Vermont's roadsides like dandelions.

Soon after Riehle was elected to Vermont's House of Representatives in 1965 and bolstered by President Johnson's Highway Beautification Act of 1965, Riehle developed a slow but steady groundswell of support for removing advertising superstructures. But the billboard-ban bill, known as "Riehle's Bill," was a hard sell that prompted hot contention in Montpelier and statewide. It was opposed by Republicans and by businesses such as car dealers and burger stands that liked the in-your-face

Interstates 89, 91, 93, and more . . . enjoy the view!

advertising option afforded them by billboards. Oddly enough, many farmers were opposed to the ban, too, because they made good money leasing their land to the billboard companies.

Although Riehle's fight was a tough one, the greener minds prevailed, and the bill passed into law in 1968, making Vermont the first state in the nation to initiate a full ban on billboard advertising. It would take a few years, but by 1974, Vermont's last billboard was removed. To date, Vermont is one of only four states to ban billboards—the other three being Alaska, Maine, and Hawaii. Not surprisingly, each of these states is famous for its natural beauty.

Amazingly, every so often some politico will try to dismantle the ban, but these attempts have thus far been quashed. Maintaining the billboard ban reveals Vermont residents' deep commitment to preserving their state's natural beauty and integrity. Ted Riehle Jr. died in 2007 at age eighty-three, on New Year's Eve, the very eve of the fortieth anniversary of his beloved billboard ban. Ironically, his legacy is a gift unseen but enjoyed by millions each day.

MICROBREWERIES

For those who like to sip, swirl, and sniff their beer—savoring, measuring, and analyzing each sip of brew—Vermont is the place to be. Those in the know call it "Vermont Beer Culture," and for good reason: The Green Mountains are positively foaming with microbreweries, brewpubs, and homebrew aficionados.

In 2006, MSNBC named Burlington the fourth best city in the world in which to enjoy a beer, just below such backwaters as Amsterdam, Berlin, and Brugge. (This designation, incidentally, makes Vermont the home of America's best beer. Ahem, ahem.) Vermont also boasts more craft breweries per capita than anywhere else in the United States.

Be it craft brew or micro brew (the difference being volume of beer produced in a given period), it all means the same thing: beer (but not the mass-produced stuff that proclaims its kingliness). When it comes to Vermont beers, we're talking handcrafted, small-batch brews made with wholesome ingredients from around the state.

Vermont's handcrafted beer movement all pretty much began on November 11, 1988. After three long years of

A brew (or two) for you?

Vermont Brewers Association: www.brewers vt.com

Vermont Brewers Festival: www.vtbrew fest.com

lobbying the state legislature to rescind outdated laws banning brewpubs (on the books since the abysmal blight known as Prohibition), Greg Noonan opened the door—and the taps—at the now famous Vermont Pub & Brewery in Burlington. He unwittingly began a trend that became an industry and a way of life that grows larger every year in Vermont, the ripple effects of which are felt globally.

Now, a quarter century later, the Green Mountain State sports dozens of brewpubs and breweries, including Zero Gravity, Long Trail, Otter Creek, Magic Hat, Trout River, Harpoon, and counting. There are also several beer festivals, most notably the not-to-be-missed Vermont Brewers Festival (2012 marks its twentieth year), the Vermont Brewers Association, the Burlington Brew Tours, several stores catering to home brewing aficionados, and untold numbers of thirsty fans quaffing artful blends.

If Benjamin Franklin is correct in saying that "Beer is proof that God loves us and wants us to be happy," then Vermont is, indeed, God's country—a heavenly place filled with tasty libation. Cheers!

BACK ROADS

Back roads, by definition, are secondary roads—which in Vermont means most unpaved roads. And Vermont has nine thousand miles of rural roads. That's a whole lot of exploring just waiting to happen. Vermont's back roads spider-web throughout the prettiest back country the state has to offer. While it is possible to get lost on them, you also have the freedom to follow your nose to see where you end up. That way, you're not lost; you're just not sure where you are.

Take the Creek Road that runs, in part, through Irasburg to Craftsbury for a winding drive through some of Vermont's prettiest country any time of year, though high summer and fall are particular standouts. Then again, mud season conjures up its own special superlatives. . . .

Vermont Resource Conservation and Development Council even has a "Better Back Roads" program that helps improve water quality by preventing road erosion and ditch runoff, a constant and expensive struggle in maintaining secondary roads. It's especially expensive in a state that has so many miles of back

Pack a lunch and follow your nose!

country with single-track lanes leading to hill farms, long-forgotten beaver ponds, and little-known hiking trails.

Some back roads offer pretty roadside picnic spots or massive maples that arch over the road, in the autumn creating a colorful canopy unmatched anywhere else. Many back roads bisect large stretches of waving green fields, which, during haying season, thrum with activity. Other back roads dip down into shady valleys and cross seemingly forgotten bridges over amber rivers and shading pristine fishing spots. Dead-end roads can offer surprising views, hidden vistas, and charming picnic spots.

Wherever you travel, make sure not to trespass on private property, or you may come face-to-face with a few irate farm dogs who haven't had a good chase since the last flatlander beat a hasty retreat.

The best way to find a Vermont back road is to get off a highway, seek out an unpaved stretch, and follow your nose. Inevitably you'll end up somewhere, and anywhere in Vermont is better than anywhere else.

DAIRY FARMS

A herd of cows grazing knee-deep in lush green grass in front of a red barn with rolling hills in the background is as much an iconic image of Vermont as a lobster dinner is to Maine. In fact, in 1930, Vermont had more cows than people: 421,000 bovines to 359,000 humans. With the commercialism that followed World War II, dairy farming became a bigger business than ever. Those were boom years for Vermont dairying—in 1947, Vermont had 11,206 dairy farms, and cows dotted the hillsides.

But for every up there is a down, and today Vermont has fewer than 1,000 dairy farms, though herd sizes have more than doubled in the past few decades to an average of 130 cows per farm. While soda pop hasn't yet ousted milk as Vermont's official state drink, the state's bovine population has been dwindling for decades. Today, there are approximately 120,000 cows and 625,471 people in Vermont.

Over the years, farmers' expenses have soared in disproportion to their incomes, while taxes and regulations have increased, making it difficult to maintain multi-generational farms

Welcome to cow country!

Strolling of the Heifers: www.strolling oftheheifers.com

Vermont Dairy Promotion Council: www.vermont dairy.com

whose beautiful historic red barns visitors expect to see. In 2011, Vermont dairy farmers were paid an average of $1.69 per gallon of milk produced, but it cost them $1.40 to produce that gallon. Despite this, they bring in $68 million per year in local and state tax revenue, and Vermont milk pumps approximately $1 million a day back into the state's economy.

Vermont's dairy heritage and industry is supported by Brattleboro's annual Dairy Festival weekend, with its famous Strolling of the Heifers parade.

Billings and Shelburne Farms are helping to spearhead a new wave in Vermont farming through encouraging the support of locally produced dairy goods straight from Vermont farms, earning $560 million and providing 7,500 jobs. Though the majority of dairy farms in Vermont are cow dairies, an increasing number are sheep and goat dairies. These non-bovine dairy farms help make it more possible than it has been for half a century to buy tasty goods from that small farm just down the road rather than someplace out of state. Now that's progress.

THE GREEN MOUNTAINS

In 1777, Revolutionary War patriot Dr. Thomas Young, a participant in the Boston Tea Party, suggested naming the state after the verdant mountains dominating the region by combining the French words for green (*verde*) and mountains (*monts*). Thankfully, the Constitutional Convention liked his idea; otherwise, the state would now be called New Connecticut. Egads.

The 250-mile-long, north–south spine of rolling hills known as the Green Mountains exists wholly within Vermont's borders. It makes up a northeast section of the Appalachian Mountains, a 1,500-mile-long range stretching from Alabama to Quebec. Some 460 million years ago, the Appalachians were the highest mountains on Earth. (Take that, Himalayas!) Today, the Green Mountains top out at Mt. Mansfield's 4,395 feet—the highest point in Vermont—and sport a dozen peaks that rise above 3,400 feet. Not bad for a genteel old mountain chain.

The green in the Green Mountains is the southern finger of a massive *biome* (dense boreal forest) that covers much of the chain. This is all a fancy way of

Green Mountain National Forest: www.fs.usda.gov/ greenmountain

saying that Vermont has more than her share of evergreens, including conifers such as spruce, pine, fir, and cedar—more than ever, in fact. Today, Vermont is 78 percent forested, with 4.46 million acres in tree growth, compared with the mid-nineteenth century, when approximately 80 percent of the state's land was open, having been cleared for agricultural uses.

The Greens still define the current residents of this place by forcing them to work hard for the privilege of living here, much as they did the Abenaki, Mohican, and Pennacook Indians for thousands of years. The Greens are home to all manner of nonhumans, too, including beaver, white-tailed deer, moose, numerous bird species, and even a few colonies of *Crotalus horridus,* the protected Eastern timber rattler, Vermont's only venomous snake.

Whether flying over the Green Mountains or hiking, biking, driving, camping, or fishing in them, it is important to cherish, marvel at, and respect these ancient rolling hills, for they are the heart and soul of Vermont—the spiritual, physical, and economic bosom of the state proudly named for them.

TOWN COMMONS

Spend any amount of time behind the wheel touring Vermont, and you'll swear that every town has a village green with a gazebo, bandstand, walking paths, ball field, benches, war memorials, and a cannon or two. In truth, you wouldn't be far off the mark. And they're all worth a visit.

The idea for Vermont's greens—or town commons—originally came to the New World with settlers from Europe, where greens form the center of most villages. Originally, they were a parcel of land used as "common" grazing property, dating from a time when little open land was available in the largely forested hinterland of northern New England. Once people began carving their own homesteads from the wilderness, brick and white-painted clapboard-and-shutter structures rose up around the commons and included libraries, town halls, general stores, post offices, and churches.

Today, commons throughout the state—such as those in Tunbridge, Lyndonville, Craftsbury, Irasburg, Woodstock, Danville, Manchester, Middlebury, Chelsea, and Townshend—thrum with some form of activity each week. Events range from farmers' markets, crafts fairs, and antique fairs, to village days, church bazaars, and baseball and softball games.

Irasburg's common is one of many sporting a fine skating rink in the nippy months, while in the summer visitors on long-distance bicycle tours collapse under its shade trees. Craftsbury is home to one of the most picturesque (aren't they all?) and certainly one of the most photographed commons in the state. Each July for more than forty years, the Craftsbury Antiques and Uniques festival hosts more than one hundred vendors and craftspeople.

The little town of Bristol, in Addison County, boasts a summer concert series by its own Bristol Band in the gazebo on the green, a melodious tradition ongoing since just after the Civil War. Some towns, including Chelsea, actually sport twin greens.

Town commons continue to be the heart of villages throughout the state. These picturesque greens provide spaces for quiet contemplation, a leisurely stroll, a game of chess, a shady spot to read, and a place for children to play, while, all around, daily life goes on at its own pace.

Greens are good for you!

Craftsbury: www.townofcraftsbury.com

Irasburg: www.irasburgvt.com

Bristol: www.bristolvt.net

COVERED BRIDGES

There are 2,600 bridges in the state of Vermont, but only 106 of them are of the covered variety. Though two dozen states have covered bridges, Vermont boasts the highest number per square mile of anywhere in the United States.

But why cover a bridge in the first place? The simple answer is: to keep the trusswork dry. The vast majority of Vermont's covered bridges were built between 1820 and 1905, by hand and of wood, making them a dear investment in both time and materials. By roofing them, those early builders hoped to extend their bridges' lives by forty years. Their logic proved sound, though modest: The Great Eddy Bridge, built in Waitsfield in 1833, is the oldest operating covered bridge in Vermont and is still very much with us.

Covered bridges were often referred to as "kissing bridges," because in the horse and buggy days, young courting couples would frequently slow their steeds and engage in a little passionate necking under cover of the bridge. Vermont is also home to two so-called "double-barreled" covered bridges,

Vermont Covered Bridge Society: www.vermont bridges.com

which accommodate two lanes of traffic flow, as well as six covered bridges built specifically for trains.

Thirteen of Vermont's fourteen counties have at least one covered bridge, and many Vermont towns are home to multiple covered bridges, such as Pittsford with four, Lyndon with five, and Tunbridge with five. The longest covered bridge within the state is the West Dummerston Bridge, at 269 feet, spanning the West River. And at 49 feet, the relatively short Emily's Bridge, in Stowe, is said to be haunted by the ghost of a young woman jilted by her lover. The 151-foot Bartonsville covered bridge, built in 1870 to span the Williams River, was on the US National Register of Historic Places, but succumbed to statewide flash flooding resulting from Hurricane Irene on August 28, 2011. It is expected to be rebuilt with traditional trusswork.

Whether recent replacements or genuine historic structures, Vermont's covered bridges can't help but bring a smile to the faces of locals and tourists alike as they steal a kiss and clop-clop-clop on through.

BEN & JERRY'S ICE CREAM

Way back in 1977, two best friends, Ben Cohen and Jerry Greenfield, took a correspondence course in ice-cream making. Bolstered by their newfound skills, they went into business for themselves. . . . And the rest, as they say, is (sweet) history.

So ubiquitous is the toothsome treat known the world over as Ben & Jerry's Ice Cream that it has flown into orbit on the US Space Shuttle and sailed the world's oceans on cruise ships. Official Ben & Jerry Scoop Shops are spread all over the world, offering cups and cones in such far-from-Vermont places as Gibraltar, Singapore, and Turkey.

One of the most visited hotspots in Vermont, by tourists and locals alike, is the Ben & Jerry's Factory in Waterbury. There, visitors can shed a tear in the Flavor Graveyard, a resting place for dearly departed flavors (Rainforest Crunch, RIP) before touring the factory. Free samples aside, no one leaves hungry from this plant that cranks out 250,000 pints a day, two flavors at once. Yum yum.

Speaking of flavors, how about a scoop of Red Velvet Cake, Chunky Monkey, Chubby Hubby, Cherry

Just one lick . . .

Ben & Jerry's Ice Cream: www.benjerry .com

Ben & Jerry's Foundation: www.benand jerrysfoundation .org

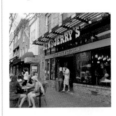

In memory of
RAINFOREST. CRUNCH
With aching heart & heavy sigh
We bid Rainforest Crunch goodbye.
That nutty brittle from exotic places
Got sticky in between our braces.
1989-1996

Garcia, Milk & Cookies, Coffee Heath Bar Crunch, Karamel Sutra, or New York Super Fudge Chunk? Or the 14,000-calorie sundae-in-a-bucket Vermonster? And let's not forget Free Cone Day, usually coinciding with Earth Day, when one million free cones, cups, and Peace Pops are given away.

In 2000, Ben and Jerry sold Ben & Jerry's Homemade Holdings, Inc., to the British–Dutch food conglomerate Unilever. Though the pair was chided at the time for selling out, Unilever continues to operate the company as a tasty instrument for positive social change. Ben & Jerry's remains firmly footed in Vermont, with its corporate offices in South Burlington and its primary manufacturing plant in Waterbury. And the milk used to make Ben & Jerry's ice cream is still purchased from Vermont farmers.

The two founding partners now run Ben & Jerry's Foundation, awarding two million dollars in grant money annually to organizations involved in progressive social change. Who knew that a correspondence course could end up making so many people all over the world so very happy?

TUNBRIDGE WORLD'S FAIR

Tunbridge always seems to be a step ahead of many other quaint Vermont villages. Not only does it have a deep and storied past, it also boasts three village centers and five covered bridges. But it is best known for its annual four-day, mid-September event known as the Tunbridge World's Fair.

The Tunbridge Fair has been called a whole lot of things in its more than 140-year history . . . among them the "wildest," "drunkest," and "raunchiest" fair in the state. Though the fair's handlers (Friends of the Tunbridge Fair) are justifiably proud of the fair's rowdy past, most of those colorful descriptors have dropped quietly away over the past few years in favor of a more scrubbed image. Even the peep shows are a thing of the past.

Founded in 1867, the fair has been held on its present site in the center of Tunbridge and hosted by the Union Agricultural Society since 1875. It earned its "World's Fair" status early on when Lieutenant Governor Burnham Martin called it a "little World's Fair." Begun as an agricultural event, the fair is still very much a celebration of local rural life. The fair has been held annually since its launch,

See you at the fair, ayuh!

1 Fairgrounds Lane, Tunbridge www.tunbridge worldsfair.com

interrupted only by the great influenza epidemic of 1918 and World War II.

The fairgrounds are home to the only remaining grass race track in the state of Vermont—which comes in handy: The fair has been a member of the National Trotting Association since 1894, and it is known for its horse racing. In addition to grandstand shows, the midway, and the Livestock Cavalcade, this wee world's fair also features cattle judging, Civil War reenactors, pig races, egg candling, contra dancers, shingle and cider making, and ox, horse, and pony pulling.

Competition is fierce among the more than five hundred entries in the Crafts and Floral category, which includes baking, canning, quilting, and pickling. And the cutthroat Harvest and Garden exhibitors compete with everything from dry beans to watermelons and half-ton pumpkins.

Since the Tunbridge World's Fair is nonprofit, all proceeds go toward making sure the town's most popular annual event continues to be anticipated by people from all over the world . . . and from just up the road.

CATAMOUNTS

The Pacific Northwest has sasquatch, Florida has its skunk ape, and Vermont has . . . the catamount, aka "cat o' the mountains"—or what outsiders call the Eastern cougar, puma, panther, or mountain lion. Problem is, the last catamount in Vermont was shot more than a century ago. But rumor has it they're back—or are they?

The pages of Vermont history abound with stories involving the 150-pound creatures. But in March 2011, the Vermont Fish and Wildlife Department declared catamounts, that long-recognized symbol of the Green Mountain State's wild past, as officially extinct in the state and likely been since the 1930s. The last—and largest—recognized specimen was shot in Barnard by Vermont farmer Alexander Crowell on Thanksgiving Day, 1881. It weighed 182 ½ pounds and measured seven feet from nose to tail tip. (It's on display at the Vermont Historical Society in Montpelier.)

So how to explain the fifty-plus sightings each year, in Vermont and in neighboring regions, of very large, tawny-colored, long-tailed cats?

Get a glimpse of the big cats!

Vermont Historical Society: www.vermont history.org

Fairbanks Museum and Planetarium: www.fairbanks museum.org

Despite the fact that the state doesn't officially recognize the catamounts reentry into civilized Vermont society, all manner of Vermont products, businesses, and organizations sport the word "catamount," including Catamount Beer, the Catamount Trail, and Catamount Health, and the University of Vermont's official mascot is a big-headed, rabble-rousing catamount known as Rally Cat.

Among the wealth of fascinating offerings at the Fairbanks Museum in St. Johnsbury is a stuffed catamount, much like the one in the 1770s that the Green Mountain Boys affixed to the signpost at their favorite watering hole, the Catamount Tavern, as a warning to land-grabbing enemies. Though the tavern burned in 1871, the Bennington hotspot is marked with a copper catamount on a base of Vermont granite. There's just one problem: the statue isn't of a catamount; it's an African lioness, the closest thing to a catamount that could be found at the time. Waste note, want not: When the statue arrived, the tuft of hair at the tip of the tail was chiseled off: instant catamount!

SHELBURNE FARMS & INN

In 1886, the well-heeled Dr. William Seward and his wife, Lila Vanderbilt Webb, bought farmland along the shore of Lake Champlain with the express notion of creating a "model agricultural estate." Famed landscape architect Frederick Law Olmstead and structure architect Robert H. Robertson were brought in to ensure that the massive estate—3,800 acres by 1902—was used to its maximum potential.

By the turn of the century, the couple's grand vision had reached its zenith, and Shelburne Farms employed three hundred workers, all toiling feverishly to keep up with the demands of the farm, which was fast becoming the foremost model agricultural estate in the nation. By the mid-twentieth century, increased operating expenses and decreased revenues forced the founders' descendents to rethink the size and scope of Shelburne Farms. In 1972, they formed an overseeing nonprofit devoted to conservation education.

The massive estate, now a National Historic Landmark, has been winnowed to 1,400 acres, but this working farm and museum is still very much a leader

Step back to the future at Shelburne Farms and Inn
1611 Harbor Road, Shelburne
www.shelburnefarms.org

in the field of agriculture. With ninety-six solar panels on the premises, it earns its title as an educational center, offering a number of programs for school children and adults. The farm produces award-winning cheddar cheese from the milk of its famous herd of Brown Swiss cows. In addition, Shelburne Farms runs a sustainable forestry program, and the seven-acre gardens provide produce for sale at farmer's markets and for use by the inn's tony restaurant.

The Inn at Shelburne Farms was once the grand nineteenth-century country home of the farm's founders. Restored in 1987, it is now a spacious, elegant, twenty-four-room hotel with four guest cottages and a world-class restaurant. One need not be a guest to dine at the inn, but the opportunity to roam the farm's extensive and endlessly compelling grounds promises an unforgettable stay.

Shelburne Farms and Inn is a renewed version of the founders' original dream, and in many ways it has surpassed that grand vision on its way to becoming something much more impressive, sustainable, and useful for everyone.

SHELBURNE MUSEUM

Just as Shelburne Farms was the brainchild of Dr. William Seward and his wife, Lila Vanderbilt Webb, the renowned Shelburne Museum is the brainchild of their daughter-in-law, art maven Electra Havemeyer Webb. From bold, not-so-humble beginnings, Shelburne Museum has long been regarded as one of America's great museums of art and Americana—and for excellent reasons.

Visitors are faced with the enviable conundrum: Where to start? The grounds themselves are stunning, offering thirty-nine galleries, historic houses, community buildings, and other surprising structures—twenty-five of which were relocated to the grounds from locations throughout Vermont—including the historic landlocked steamboat *Ticonderoga*. Plus, there's a lighthouse, an apothecary, a blacksmith shop, a railroad station (complete with locomotive), a round barn, a covered bridge, a jailhouse, a carousel, and more . . . much more.

It's not hyperbole to say that's not the half of it. The structures contain some of the world's finest examples of

The past is alive and well at Shelburne Museum 6000 Shelburne Road, Shelburne www.shelburne museum.org

art and Americana assembled anywhere, including folk art, quilts, decoys, carriages, circus figures, posters, toys, dolls and dollhouses, tools, decorative arts, and dare we say . . . more? Happily, yes.

The paintings collection includes important works by French Impressionists and more than four hundred eighteenth- through twentieth-century American artworks, including paintings by Winslow Homer, Fitz Hugh Lane, Grandma Moses, Carl Rungius, Andrew Wyeth, and many others.

The grounds at Shelburne Museum are home to two dozen gardens that, like their structural counterparts, bear names and functions, many historical. There are kitchen gardens, herb gardens, an heirloom vegetable garden, and an apothecary garden, as well as four hundred lilac trees, 1,700 daylilies in thirty-eight varieties, peonies, and many other horticultural delights, all maintained organically.

Inside and out, Shelburne Museum is a vibrant, living repository of history, architecture, gardens, art, and Americana. You'll be hard-pressed to find someone who's bored there.

LITERARY TRADITION

There must be something in the water. Otherwise, why would so many fine writers either hail from, be drawn to, or spend formative time in Vermont?

Dummerston, close to the banks of the Connecticut River, was Rudyard Kipling's home for four years beginning in 1892. His custom-built abode still stands on Kipling Road. There Kipling wrote some of his most famous works, including *The Jungle Book*s and *Captains Courageous.*

More than a century later and at the other end of the state, award-winning author Howard Frank Mosher resides in a small town in his beloved Northeast Kingdom. It is from there that he mines that region's deep and intriguing history and traditions, remaking them to suit his singular vision. He calls his fine creation "Kingdom County," and it is the dominant, recurring character in his novels.

Robert Frost, though closely associated with New Hampshire, in fact spent his summers and falls, from 1939 to 1963, at his farm in Ripton, and he wrote many of his best-loved works there. He is buried in the Old Bennington Cemetery. Frost was also

Write on!

Howard Frank
Mosher:
www.howard
frankmosher.com

League of
Vermont Writers:
www.leagueof
vermontwriters
.org

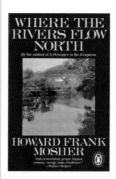

instrumental in founding the Bread Loaf Writers Conference. Established in 1926 on the campus of Middlebury College, it is the oldest and one of the most prestigious writers' conferences in America.

Plainfield's Goddard College is home of the nation's first low-residency MFA in creative writing program, which has had among its alumni and faculty Walter Mosley, Raymond Carver, and David Mamet. The long-standing League of Vermont Writers was established in 1929.

The long list of authors associated with Vermont includes poets, playwrights, nonfiction writers, memoirists, children's authors, literary writers, mystery writers, science fiction authors—and even writers of Westerns. Some of the many standouts include: Chris Bohjalian, Archer Mayor, Tasha Tudor, David Budbill, Grace Paley, Joseph Citro, Garret Keizer, John Irving, Jay Parini, Bill McKibben, Ruth Stone, Robert E. Pike, Shirley Jackson, Galway Kinnell, Reeve Lindbergh, Julia Alvarez, Piers Anthony, Pearl S. Buck, Aleksandr Solzhenitsyn, Michael A. Stackpole, D. Kurt Singer, James Hayford, and no doubt, many more to come.

"NAULAHKA"
Rudyard Kipling's Home near Brattleboro for 4 Years
...
After marriage to the American, Caroline Balestier, and after visiting her home, famed British writer built isolated "Naulahka". Here he wrote the "Jungle Books" and other stories, and two daughters were born. In 1896 the Kiplings returned to England.
PRIVATE HOME.   WEST 2 MILES.
VERMONT HISTORIC SITES COMMISSION

Bread Loaf
Mountain
Campus

MIDDLEBURY COLLEGE

ROBERT LEE FROST
MAR. 26, 1874 ~ JAN. 29, 1963
"I HAD A LOVER'S QUARREL WITH THE WORLD"

HIS WIFE
ELINOR MIRIAM
25, 1873 ~

THE LONG TRAIL

The Long Trail is the oldest long-distance hiking trail in the United States, and at 273 miles, it more than lives up to its plain-Jane moniker. The trail stretches north–south along the Green Mountains from the Vermont/Massachusetts border near Williamstown to the Vermont/Canada border at North Troy, wending and winding its way along Vermont's highest peaks.

One can't mention the Long Trail without also mentioning the Green Mountain Club, for their histories are the same. In 1909, outdoor enthusiast James P. Taylor had a monumental idea while watching the mist rise from atop Stratton Mountain, inspiring him to form the Green Mountain Club (GMC). This nonprofit organization was created specifically to construct Vermont's "footpath in the wilderness" as well as to maintain and protect the Long Trail for all to enjoy for generations to come.

The Long Trail was also the inspiration for the longer Appalachian Trail, and the two trails share terrain through Vermont. The Inn

Take a hike!

Green Mountain Club:
www.greenmountainclub.org

Inn at Long Trail:
www.innatlongtrail.com

at Long Trail, in Killington, sits at the spot where the Long and Appalachian Trails diverge. Since 1938, the rustic bed and breakfast has catered to hikers, whose notes of thanks festoon the walls. This alpine oasis is the best place on the trail for hikers to kick back and enjoy a burger and a frosty bottle of Long Trail Ale by Vermont's own Long Trail Brewing Company.

Today, the GMC has more than 9,500 members, one thousand of whom volunteer to maintain the trail system. The club is officially recognized by the Vermont State Legislature as "the founder, sponsor, defender, and protector" of the Long Trail System. The GMC also publishes handbooks and maps and protects the Long Trail where it crosses private land. Thus far in its Long Trail Protection Campaign, the GMC has protected 24,500 acres (and counting). As the anti-interstate, the Long Trail offers one of the finest ways to see Vermont—by hiking history atop her mountains. It beats the heck out of half-seeing her from inside a speeding car.

THE MORGAN HORSE

Morgans—the Swiss Army knife of equines—have been known to hunt, jump, race, plow fields, and haul sap and logs. They can pull carriages and be ridden cowboy style or English style, and they've carried policemen and soldiers at war. In fact, the Morgan is the official horse of the US Cavalry. Oh, and this first officially recognized American horse breed does it all with a smile. Yep, they smile. Is there anything a Morgan can't do?

The foundation sire of the Morgan breed is Figure, born in Springfield, Massachusetts (oh dear), in 1789, and later owned by a Massachusetts farmer and singing instructor, Justin Morgan, who thankfully settled in Tunbridge, Vermont. As Figure grew, he became noted for his uncanny versatility, muscular build, and friendly temperament—not to mention his impressive ability to pass along his strong genes—traits that carry through the Morgan line to this day.

Vermont is home to many Morgan-centric organizations that all work toward the same end: to promote, preserve, and improve the Morgan horse

University of Vermont Morgan Horse Farm: www.uvm.edu/ morgan

Vermont Morgan Horse Association: www.vtmorgan horse.com

breed. Among them are the American Morgan Horse Association, based in Shelburne; the National Museum of the Morgan Horse, in Middlebury; and the Vermont Morgan Horse Association, organized in 1966 to promote and celebrate the breed.

The most prominent Morgan institution is the University of Vermont's Morgan Horse Farm, in Weybridge, which, for the past half century has worked to improve Morgans through careful breeding and selection. The impressive facility, listed on the National Register of Historic Places, runs a popular apprentice program and is open for tours from May through October. Each fall the program raffles a lovely Morgan foal in a popular two-dollar-per-ticket drawing.

People who know about such things say that the Morgan horse epitomizes grace, beauty, stamina, reliability, versatility, and loyalty. As it happens, you'll find that Vermonters quietly espouse these same traits, so it makes perfect sense that the Morgan is also Vermont's official state animal.

VERMONT TEDDY BEAR COMPANY

In 1981, John Sortino was shocked to find that none of his young son's teddy bears were made in the USA. Within two years, Sortino was selling his own homemade bears from a pushcart in Burlington's Church Street Marketplace. Then, a customer asked to have a bear mailed to her, and the idea of the Bear-Gram was born. Soon, Sortino was mailing teddy bears all over the world—especially on Valentine's Day. By 1990, Sortino's company was ranked the eightieth fastest-growing privately held company in America, the next year, it became the fifty-sixth.

Every Vermont Teddy Bear Factory bear is designed, cut, sewn, stuffed, and stitched at one of two Vermont factories—in Shelburne and Newport—that, together, produce between 350,000 and 500,000 teddy bears each year. The fuzzy friends come in various styles, sizes, colors, and themes and bedecked in all manner of garb and disguise, from biker gear to nurse, fisherman, ballerina . . . and a plain old bear.

In order to accommodate the 150,000 people it welcomes each year

Make a new friend at The Vermont Teddy Bear Factory 6655 Shelburne Rd., Shelburne; www.vermont teddybear.com

(making it the fourth most-visited attraction in Vermont), the Vermont Teddy Bear Factory at Shelburne is open seven days a week, year-round, except for Christmas, Easter, Thanksgiving, and New Year's Day. Guided tours take thirty minutes, but visitors really need at least an hour to get the full furry vibe and to "Make a Friend for Life." Literally.

For a modest $19.99, visitors can stuff a thirteen-inch bear, pop in a little red heart, sew up the bear, choose a name, and tote off their newly built bruin in a special travel case (complete with air holes). If a visit's out of the question, highly trained "Bear Counselors" make the long-distance custom-bear-creation process painless.

All Vermont Teddy Bears are unconditionally guaranteed for life. If a teddy bear should get a little too much lovin' or unwanted attention from the other family friend (aka the dog), bears sent to the Factory's "Bear Hospital" can be nursed back to their prime by one of the 160 employees, a little patience, and a steady intravenous drip of premium Vermont honey.

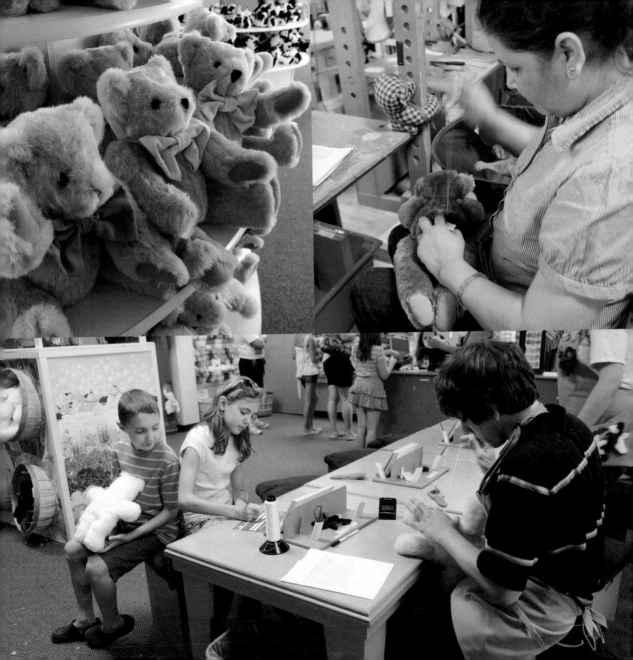

FIDDLEHEADS

Every April and May, a wave of yearning for *Matteuccia struthiopteris* threatens to overcome Vermonters young and old. The emergence from the muddy earth of the tender, tasty furled baby ostrich fern known as the fiddlehead signals spring's arrival to the Green Mountain State.

Fiddleheads are a seasonal food that grow wild in a wide range of northern regions all over the world, but in eastern and northeastern parts of North America, the ostrich fern grows in abundance. Each state or province lays claim to being the nexus of all that is fiddleheads, though they appear to be particularly fruitful in Vermont's Northeast Kingdom.

Native Americans first taught white European settlers how to gather this short-lived delicacy. Now, fiddleheading is an annual tradition that finds many Vermont families heading on out to wet areas, such as the banks of rivers, ponds, and streams as well as semi-shaded spots in the woods that offer the tender plants adequate moisture levels. The tightly furled fronds of a young fern resemble the scrolled head of a violin, and this gives fiddleheads their name.

Pick 'em up at your local farmstand or farmer's market: www.vermont agriculture.com/ buylocal/buy

But ostrich fern fiddleheads differ visually from other types of ferns that also grow locally. Most other varieties of ferns found in Vermont are inedible and contain carcinogens that can cause illness.

Ostrich fern fiddleheads are harvested when the plant is young and no more than a couple of inches above ground, while the fronds are still tight and unfurled. The brown papery husk is brushed off, and the fiddleheads are washed well and then boiled or sautéed. Cooked right (and served with melted butter, vinegar, perhaps a little garlic), fiddleheads taste like spinach or asparagus. They are also a fine source of nutrients, packed with potassium, vitamin C, iron, fiber, niacin, and Omegas 3 and 6, and they have antioxidant properties. Many folks freeze them, but pickling is the most popular method of preserving the tasty morsels.

Tagging along with a seasoned fiddleheader is the best way to learn the locations of the best fiddlehead patches, well-kept secrets passed down in families through generations. If this all sounds a bit covert, it could be you haven't had a plate of well-prepared fiddleheads lately.

JOHNSON WOOLEN MILLS

Thanks in large part to Johnson Woolen Mills' dedication to its time-tested classic styles, Vermonters still know the inherent value of a good wool garment. Despite the advent of high-tech trousers, the same heavy duty, twenty-eight-ounce, green wool pants made by this mill a century ago are still made in Johnson and still in vogue, providing unmatched warmth to new generations of folks, among them snowboarders, cross-country skiers, and of course, fishermen and hunters.

Stacy Barrows Manosh, the fourth-generation owner of Johnson Woolen Mills, is exceedingly proud of her family's long Vermont lineage, which stretches back to the 1790s, when her ancestors from England settled in Irasburg as farmers. In 1907, her great-grandfather bought out mill owner I. L. Pearl, changed the business name to Johnson Woolen Mills (JWM), and they were off and running.

Though a new building was built in the mid-1980s, right next to the old 1842 mill (still in use as the company store and visitors' center), all JWM

For all that's woolly and warm, visit Johnson Woolen Mills 51 Lower Main Street East, Johnson www.johnson woolenmills.com

manufacturing is still done the old-fashioned way. In a room the length of a football field, fabrics are marked and cut by hand on a fifty-foot-long cutting table before being passed along to the next crew of workers. Along the way and in true frugal Vermonter fashion, all scraps are gathered and later made into mittens, hot pads, and other handy items.

Johnson Woolen Mills continues to make its best-selling traditional products, including its perennially popular "Hunting Coat," a thick, rugged affair made for the rigors of an outdoorsy lifestyle. Although the mill uses some century-old patterns for many of its longtime traditional favorites, JWM is no stodgy nostalgia ride.

In addition to offering its own new lines of stylish togs for women and kids, JWM also manufactures goods for larger retail brands. In recent years, Johnson Woolen Mills has seen a dramatic increase in orders for wool outerwear from Japan. It seems that Vermonters aren't the only ones who know about the many benefits of wearing wool from head to toe.

APPLES

Call 'em what they will—winter bananas in colonial times and the official state fruit today—Vermonters harbor a fondness for apples that goes far beyond passion and for good reason. Apples are healthful to the max, packing more than 1,500 milligrams of vitamin C into a single fruit. A medium-size apple offers a meager eighty calories and zilch on the sodium and cholesterol charts. And it's been found that the regular ingestion of apples improves lung function and may help reduce the risks of cancers and strokes.

Apples fit in the hand, and no matter the size of the person, there's an apple to accommodate each waiting palm. They shine up beautifully and look stunning, and no two are alike. Apples also keep well for long periods, and they can be made into other tasty treats, such as pies (Vermont's official state pie, by the way, is . . . yep, apple), sauces, and ciders (hard and sweet!).

Speaking of cider, the Cold Hollow Cider Mill in Waterbury is the preeminent spot in Vermont for old-fashioned cider pressed as you

Get to the core of the matter:

Vermont Apple Marketing Board: www.vermont apples.org

Cold Hollow Cider Mill: www.coldhollow .com

Woodchuck Hard Cider: www.woodchuck .com

watch, seven days a week, year-round. And their cider donuts go great with a cup of hot mulled cider. If you prefer cider with a kick, scout up a bottle or six of Woodchuck Hard Cider, found wherever lip-smacking beverages are sold.

Seventy percent of Vermont's annual apple crop are McIntosh, because they are hardy, tasty, and among the easiest of keepers. But they are hardly the only variety found in the fall hereabouts. Among the dozens of standard and heirloom varieties grown in the Green Mountain State are Cortlands, Macouns, Red Delicious, and Empire—and the list could go on for pages.

Vermont's 4,000 acres of commercial apple crops annually produce more than 9 billion pounds of fruit that bring in $1.57 billion in tourism revenue. And in a state renowned for its dedication to the old ways, especially where agricultural pursuits are concerned, it should come as no surprise that at every one of Vermont's commercial orchards, each winter banana is handpicked.

QUECHEE BALLOON FESTIVAL

Look! Up in the sky! It's a bird, it's a plane! Nope, it's a hot-air balloon. A couple dozen of them, in fact. June 17–19, 2011 marked the thirty-second anniversary of the Quechee Balloon Festival, the longest continuously running hot-air balloon festival in New England—and the one with the prettiest surroundings.

Visited by more than 100,000 people each year, the festival is held alongside the 165-foot-deep, 13,000-year-old Quechee Gorge—Vermont's deepest, called the "Grand Canyon of Vermont." Quechee village is designated on the National Register of Historic Places and is home to two eighteen-hole golf courses, polo grounds, Scottish games, and more.

Like exhaling dragons snorting flame and lifting skyward, the festival's mammoth balloons fill to near-bursting with fire and air heated by propane burners and rise silently through tendrils of fog curling in the lowlands, over the lush green Upper Valley of the Quechee region. The balloons seem to appear with an unnerving suddenness, but once spied, they never fail to draw a smile and a wishful look from the land-bound masses.

Up, up, and away!

Quechee Balloon, Craft, and Music Festival: www.quechee balloonfestival .com

Because so much of the art of hot-air ballooning depends on factors controlled by Mother Nature, such as temperature, precipitation, wind, and the threat of lightning, an event such as the Quechee Balloon Festival is a dicey undertaking. Yet, people have flocked to this three-day family event for more than thirty years—where these days they also enjoy music, a climbing wall, bungee jumping, parachutist demonstrations, more than sixty crafters and vendors, and a wine and beer garden for the adults. If the weather cooperates, at dusk the gathered balloons huff skyward into the twilight in a stunning spectacle known as Balloon Glow.

Rides in tethered balloons are available, and for $225 per person, attendees can experience the thrill of a full out, untethered hot-air balloon trip. The two-hour experience isn't inexpensive, but the singular sensation of floating a thousand feet above the earth in complete silence, looking down on some of the prettiest terrain in Vermont, is as unforgettable as it is addictive. Fortunately, the Quechee Balloon Festival shows no sign of being grounded.

SKIING

Come November, with barely a respite following the tail end of the spectacular fall foliage season, Vermont's roads once again hum with cars of people heading for the hills—this time in search of the white stuff, their luggage racks packed with skis, poles, and boots (and with snowboards and snowshoes!).

Vermont's forty-one world-class ski resorts, strung along the Green Mountains chain like jewels on the neck of a fair-skinned heiress, attract hordes of both Nordic (cross country) and alpine (downhill) skiers. Vermont's one thousand ski trails covering six thousand acres receive more than 225 inches of snow each season.

Killington Resort, the largest ski area in the east, offers eighty-seven miles of trails that accommodate every skill level, from toddler to old pro. Meanwhile, Jay Peak sits at the top of the state and at the top of the list of family-favorite resorts. Stowe Mountain Resort, on Mt. Mansfield, the highest mountain in the state at 4,395 feet, offers 118 trails. It's also the home mountain of the University of Vermont's ski team. Speaking of Stowe, smack in the heart of the

Time to hit the slopes!

Vermont Ski Areas Association: www.skivermont .com

Vermont Ski Museum: www.vermont skimuseum.org

Catamount Trail: www.catamount trail.org

state's skiing-est town sits the Vermont Ski Museum, a repository of Vermont's slope-centric history. But it's Woodstock that's home to the nation's first ski tow.

The long and impressive list of great skiing spots also includes Mad River Glen, Sugarbush, Okemo, Bolton, Burke, Smuggler's Notch (aka Smuggs), Stratton, and Bromley, among others—with each ski area doing its best to outdo the rest. Numerous smaller, often overlooked operations offer great value with modest pass prices, short lift lines, and clear slopes.

The Green Mountains are home to more than forty world-class cross-country ski centers offering thousands of miles of trails, many groomed, including those at Bolton Valley and Craftsbury Nordic Center. The Trapp Family Lodge, home of the first cross-country ski center in the country, offers a one-hundred-kilometer network of groomed trails, and the Catamount Trail is a three-hundred-mile Nordic ski trail running the entire length of Vermont.

To most folks who hit Vermont's many slopes and meadows, skiing is not just a passion, it's a way of life.

TOWN MEETING DAY

Town Meeting Day has been a Vermont tradition since 1762, when the first was held in Bennington, long before Vermont became the fourteenth state in 1791. Always held on the first Tuesday in March, this official state holiday is an opportunity for Vermonters to practice democracy at its most basic level. Though voting on whether pigs should be allowed to roam free in town limits is no longer on most towns' agendas, many of the more than 245 Vermont towns that still hold the annual get-togethers (in town halls, school gymnasiums, and salt sheds) strive for civil discussion and debate.

State employees receive the day off with pay, and most private employees can opt to take the day off in order to attend what is usually a daytime meeting. Often the meeting is interrupted with a sit-down potluck meal—another reason why Town Meeting Day is a much-anticipated annual event. Just after pie and more coffee and while a contingent of volunteers cleans up in the kitchen, the afternoon session kicks off.

That's when discussion often turns into debate and debate into heated

Vermonters speaking their minds since 1762.

exchange, and democracy in its purest form is in full swing. Night comes early and lingers long as the moderator—charged with overseeing the meeting—raises articles, hammers them down, and sets them aside to make room for the next agenda item. All the while, it's the town clerk's job to tally votes and keep minutes of the bustling discussions.

Some communities have tried to hold their town meetings on Saturdays but have found such a change does not increase attendance, while others opt for nighttime meetings in an effort to attract larger crowds after work. Occasionally, town meetings are postponed due to inclement weather. (It is March in Vermont, after all).

Regardless, for many Vermonters town meetings are must-attend events. Where else can a single voice have such direct and immediate democratic effect on the election of local officials and the forthcoming year's budgets—line by mind-numbing line? Then there are the coffee and homemade maple sinkers (donuts). Now that's Vermont democracy in action.

BENNINGTON POTTERS

One of Bennington's many fine attributes is its location—smack dab on top of prime clay deposits and ample running water, elements vital in the production of pottery. It stands to reason that way back in 1785, Revolutionary War veteran Captain John Norton would choose Bennington as the spot to produce his redware glazed pottery. By 1804, redware had been replaced by stoneware, a more rugged compound better able to withstand the vicissitudes of daily use.

Despite such tradition, by the time a young craftsman named David Gil came to town in 1948, pottery making in Bennington had all but died out. Undaunted, Gil began making his practical, handmade stoneware offerings, and his business grew. In 1964, he moved to larger, historic buildings on 4.5 acres. As the years rolled by, Bennington Potters' reputation grew, and its offerings included a mail-order catalogue, a showroom, and retail space.

Though Gil died in 2002, at seventy-nine, Bennington Potters continues in its sixth decade with a team of apprentices and professionals hard at work. Potters Yard, the world's largest

Visit Potters Yard:

Bennington Potters 324 County Street, Bennington www.benningtonpotters.com

ongoing producer of craft pottery, hosts thousands of visitors annually—many of whom get great deals at the (Potters) Yard Sale held every summer. Each piece of Bennington pottery is handmade, so no two are alike. All pieces—including bread pans, pie pans, muffin pans, casserole dishes, canister sets, mixing bowls, and mugs—are oven, microwave, dishwasher, and food safe. It is rumored that President Obama and his family use Bennington Potters' dishware.

Bennington Potters' designs are at once bold and practical, yet soft and pleasing to the eye. Among the company's most popular offerings is the two-loop handle Trigger Mug, one of Gil's own signature designs, available in his famous storm-cloud-like spatterware patterns, three of which form Bennington Potters' "traditional" glazes: the famous Blue Agate, Black on Green, and Morning Glory Blue.

Captain Norton could not have known in 1785 that nearly 230 years later, stoneware would still be made in Bennington, but it's a good bet he would have enjoyed a drop or two from his very own Trigger Mug.

FISHING

No matter one's piscatorial passion, an angler would be hard-pressed to go anywhere in Vermont and not have a patch of water close at hand. With hundreds of public-access ponds under twenty acres in size, 288 public lakes twenty acres or larger in size, and hundreds of state-owned public access spots on rivers, the Green Mountain State is an angler's heaven.

In winter, the flat white surfaces of Vermont's ponds and lakes—such as Lake Memphremagog in the northern US–Canada border city of Newport—are speckled with pickups, snowmobiles, ice huts, and bundled-up families tending their tip-ups. Spring fishing traditionally kicks off on an early Saturday in April, aka Opening Day, perhaps best experienced below Willoughby Falls in Orleans, where Thermoses of hot coffee are as abundant as fishing rods. Upstream, spawning steelhead hurl themselves up the 125-foot series of rapids in their zeal to get to Lake Willoughby.

Way back in 1866, the state legislature appointed a Board of Fish Commissioners to help rein in rampant overfishing. Today, Vermont's clear, cold

Fish on!

Vermont Fish & Wildlife Dept.: www.vtfishand wildlife.com

The American Museum of Fly Fishing: www.amff.com

Orvis: www.orvis.com

waters are home to eighty-nine species of fish. At Vermont's west edge, one-hundred-mile-long Lake Champlain is home to landlocked salmon, while to the east, the Connecticut River is perfect for drift boating and trout fishing. Opportunities for fly-fishing in Vermont are seemingly limitless on rivers such as the Winooski, Lamoille, Black, and Missisquoi.

But it is to Manchester that fly-fishermen the world over pilgrimage to fish the Battenkill, arguably New England's most popular trout stream. While there, they visit the American Museum of Fly Fishing, which claims the world's largest collection of fly-angling art and artifacts. They also drop by the flagship store of The Orvis Company, purveyor of high-end fly-fishing, hunting, and sporting goods. Founded in 1856 by Charles F. Orvis, the company is the oldest mail-order retailer in the country.

Other places may offer bigger and more fish, but only in Vermont can you wet a line and look up between twitches to see a covered bridge, grazing cows in a green pasture, a white church steeple, and breathtaking fall color all at once.

WOODSTOCK

If ever a town was built on the impressive footing of superlatives, it is Woodstock. Called everything from "the prettiest small town in America" to the "quintessential New England village," Woodstock has earned all those accolades and more since it was first settled in 1768.

Officially, Woodstock is a composite of three villages: Woodstock, South Woodstock, and Taftsville. For a brief time, Woodstock was the state's first unofficial capital, as the Vermont General Assembly met there in 1807 prior to moving the state government's official digs to Montpelier in 1808.

Never a burg to rest on such fusty laurels, Woodstock village recently installed free Wi-Fi and made the investment to bury all of its aboveground power and phone lines to keep the town pretty. Anyone with an urge to occupy one of those postcard-perfect Georgian, Federal, or Greek Revival style homes on The Green in Woodstock had better have deep pockets, for homes in that posh neighborhood are among the most expensive real estate in Vermont.

The quintessential Vermont village: www.woodstock vt.com

But you don't have to buy a home in Woodstock to enjoy its numerous charms. Strolling Central Street brings you to Vermont's oldest independent bookstore, the Yankee Bookshop, in the book biz since 1935. The Woodstock Inn & Resort, a superior accommodation in the grand tradition of Vermont inns, is located in the heart of town. The quintessential mercantile F. H. Gillingham & Sons General Store has been selling all manner of wares to the public since 1886. While there, be sure to pick up a copy of the *Vermont Standard,* the town newspaper—nearing its 160th year.

The Ottauquechee River flows through town and is spanned by three covered bridges: Lincoln Bridge, built in 1871; Middle Bridge, a newbie built in 1969; and Taftsville Bridge, one of Vermont's oldest, built in 1836, and at 189 feet, also one of the longest.

Just out of town sits Billings Farm & Museum, established in 1871, famous for its herd of award-winning Jersey cows. Nearby is the 634-acre Marsh-Billings-Rockefeller National Historic Park, one of only two Vermont sites in the US National Park System.

ROUND BARNS

The first round barn in America was built by George Washington in 1793 at his farm in Virginia. But round barns, which include circular shaped and those with multiple sides, really came into their own with the religious community the Shakers, who approved of the shape because, they said, "the devil can't catch you in the corners."

Designed as labor-saving structures, with livestock often facing inward toward a central feeding location, round barns became popular nationally in the middle of the nineteenth century. Most of the round barns constructed in the United States were built between 1850 and 1920, with the earliest examples being octagonal in shape.

As the industrialization of the dairy industry required farmers to build longer, linear structures that could accommodate larger herds, round barns fell out of favor and their construction slowed, with the last round barn in Vermont built in 1920. Fortunately, many fine examples still exist throughout the state.

Vermont's first and one of its most handsome round barns was built in 1899 in Barnet and is still in use

Round barns 'round the state: www.dalejtravis .com/barn/barnvt .htm

The Round Barn Farm: 1661 East Warren Road, Waitsfield; www.theround barn.com

today. Shelburne Museum is home to Vermont's most-visited round barn, an eighty-foot in diameter, three-story, red structure dating from 1901. It's fully refurbished and affords visitors a glimpse of the impressive inner trusswork of a true round barn.

Many of Vermont's round barns continue to be used for their original purpose, such as the red one in Irasburg, a landmark seen for miles. Others are in use in novel ways, such as one on Grand Isle, in Lake Champlain, that has been converted into senior apartments.

Perhaps one of the most famous round barns in Vermont is at the Inn at Round Barn Farm in Waitsfield. The barn, a twelve-sided structure, dates from 1910. Restored between 1988 and 1990, it is now an inn and a go-to place for weddings.

Vermont's oldest round structure, a sixteen-sided affair, has never been a barn. It's the Round Church, built in Richmond, Chittenden County, in 1812–1814 as a meetinghouse. It predates many of the state's round barns by nearly a century, is in prime condition, and open for visits. No cows allowed.

GREEN MOUNTAIN COFFEE

In 1980, Bob Stiller sipped an eye-opening cup of java at a small coffee shop in Waitsfield. He bought into that little business, and a year later he incorporated Green Mountain Coffee Roasters (GMCR). Soon, he moved production to Waterbury, where GMCR's corporate headquarters still resides today, at 33 Coffee Lane. If it's a visit you're after, you'll want to drop by the restored Waterbury Train Station, where GMCR opened its Visitors' Center and Café in 2006.

Today, GMCR java can be found far and wide, from corporate boardrooms and mini-marts, to McDonald's and supermarkets. In fact, retail outlets aside, the bulk of Green Mountain Coffee Roaster's sales pour in from its more than eight thousand wholesale accounts.

Not satisfied with developing its own award-winning lines of coffees—flavored, organic, fair trade, and otherwise—and with breaking sales records, seemingly one after the next—GMCR has been on a buying spree over the past few years. It's been gobbling up various and diverse coffee-related lines, including Tully's Coffee, Timothy's World

Care for a cuppa?

Green Mountain Coffee Roasters Visitors' Center & Café:

1 Rotarian Place, Waterbury www.green mountaincoffee .com

Coffee, Diedrich Coffee, Caribou Coffee, and the Keurig Single-Cup Brewing System. The company also has formed a partnership with Newman's Organics and even struck a deal with rival Starbucks.

The sharp tang of a good cup of coffee is the satisfying end result of a long and labor-intensive process that began years before GMCR existed and in places far from the green hills of Vermont. The harvest of coffee beans is often a family affair, and harvest time coincides with school vacations in nearly inaccessible, though prolific, coffee-growing regions of Mexico and Tanzania. In some of those regions, GMCR has established committed, long-term relationships with its growers.

More than once, GMCR has held the top spot on the list of 100 Best Corporate Citizens. It contributes at least 5 percent of its annual pretax profits to socially responsible initiatives. If we needed any more reason to enjoy Green Mountain Coffee Roasters' blends, it helped develop an all-natural paper cup lined with a sugar-based plastic that is 100 percent renewable.

POLITICS

In 1777, delegates from twenty-eight villages and towns formed the Republic of New Connecticut (aka the Republic of the Green Mountains), becoming one of only four states to claim itself a sovereign nation. The Continental Congress declined to recognize the upstarts, but that didn't stop the rabble rousers from establishing their own currency, a coin called Vermont coppers. They also abolished slavery within their borders and allowed adult males to vote, regardless of property owned. The new republic's 1777 constitution was so well crafted that it remains in place today, with a handful of amendments.

Vermont was admitted to the Union as the fourteenth state in 1791. In 1805, the state's seat of power was established in Montpelier, still the least populated state capitol in the country. The current statehouse—the city's third and the country's smallest—was built in 1859, and its gleaming dome is covered in genuine gold flake. It is here that some of the state's most hotly debated political issues have been decided.

In 1968, residents voted to oust all billboards, one of only four states to

The home of independent thought: www.vermont.gov

ban them. In 2004–2005, irate over tax issues, Killington residents tried to secede from Vermont and join New Hampshire—twenty-five miles eastward. And you can still see "Take Back Vermont" signs statewide, a reaction to the same-sex marriage bill in 2009.

Calvin Coolidge was one of two Vermonters to occupy the Oval Office, the other being Chester A. Arthur. Neither was elected to the position.

From Ethan Allen and the Green Mountain Boys, to Stephen A. Douglas (famed abolitionist and Abraham Lincoln debater), and on to Governor-turned-Senator George Aiken (who spent $17.09 on his last reelection campaign), Governor Madeleine Kunin (Vermont's first and only female governor), Governor Howard Dean (who balanced the budget eleven times), and Senators James Jeffords (who famously switched parties from Republican to Independent), Patrick Leahy (Vermont's first and only elected Democratic US Senator), and Bernie Sanders (pictured at right; the only Socialist ever elected to the US Senate)—phew!—Vermont's political lineage has never been dull.

DOCT JONAS FAY
Author of the Declaration
of Independence of the
State of Vermont
Member & Secretary
of the Council of Safety

A.D. 1777
Died March 6, 1818
Æ 82

MUD SEASON

Here's a good one: What do you call a brown pickup truck in April in Vermont? A blue pickup the rest of the year! Mud season, aka Vermont's unofficial fifth season, shoehorned between winter and spring, can transform even the most experienced Vermonter into a fist shaker and can turn a ride on an otherwise dry back road into an all-out wrestling match with the steering wheel.

Surely, you're wondering, it can't be as bad as all that. And you'd be right . . . mostly. But there are times each spring when it seems as though the whole world is a squishy, brown place devoid of mood-enhancing color. The media reports the arrival of spring's first blooms—everywhere on earth, it seems, but Vermont. You step out of your car or truck to walk to your front door and realize too late that your wingtips and argyles are now bog boots.

Because Vermont is an inherently hilly place, early settlers tended to set up shop in the lush, low-lying regions—the verdant valleys where rich, river-bottom lands proved conducive to growing crops

Head off the highway in April . . . but don't forget your barn boots!

and pasturing farm animals. Most of the year, this plan works just fine. Come spring, however, when the winter's heavy snow begins to melt, all that water has to go somewhere. And it does: downhill, in the form of runoff, causing flooding, muddy roads, and stuck tires.

In mud season, garages, back porches, and wood rooms become mud rooms—a Vermonter's equivalent to Superman's phone booths—a coveted space for transformation. People heading out into the sucking maw of mud don their knee-high rubber barn boots and swallow audibly. They tread forth into a damp, leafless world, only to return later, exhausted, their boots unrecognizable under a stiffening layer of heavy clay gumbo.

The good news is that mud season never lasts longer than a few weeks. Eventually, the crocuses and daffodils push through, tender green grass pokes up, and gray trees force a double take, a slight green haze evident where only the morning before there was none. Well earned, spring comes to Vermont . . . at long last.

ROCK OF AGES QUARRY

Vermont's immediate neighbor to the east might call itself the Granite State, but it's in Barre, Vermont—the self-proclaimed "Granite Center of the World"—where you'll find the world's largest granite quarry, Rock of Ages. The mammoth deposit has supplied granite to the world since 1885.

Barre's granite industry was actually established shortly after the War of 1812, but it wasn't until 1875, with the arrival of train service, that the eminently useful weather-resistant rock could be transported cost-effectively over long distances. As word of the enormous granite deposit reached the world, stoneworkers from all over the globe journeyed to Barre, resulting in a massive influx of nationalities and an increase in population from 2,000 in 1880 to 12,000 by 1894.

The source of that attraction was a deposit of rich granite that geologists claim is two miles wide, four miles long, and ten miles deep. At the rate of present consumption, there is a 4,500-year supply of Barre gray, the most popular color, yet to quarry.

Rock of Ages:
558 Graniteville
Road, Graniteville
www.rockof
ages.com

Barre Granite
Association:
www.barre
granite.org

Since 1924, visitors have been touring Rock of Ages, which is located in, appropriately enough, Graniteville (aka East Barre). From a viewing platform, the hardy can peer six hundred feet down into the curiously carved chasm to watch quarriers cut and haul slabs of raw granite with cranes capable of lifting 250 tons. Self-guided tours of the nearby 160,000-square foot factory aren't complete without a go on the outdoor granite bowling alley.

One-third of the gravestones and mausoleums in the United States come from Barre, so it stands to reason that the town's ironically named Hope Cemetery reveals some of the world's most creative headstones. Rock of Ages granite also can be found supporting and decorating some of the world's most impressive monuments and structures, including Bountiful Temple in Salt Lake City, Utah; Island Center Plaza in Hong Kong, China; and the Museum of the American Indian and Smithsonian Institution in Washington, DC. And, of course, the Vermont State Capitol building in Montpelier features (what else?) Barre gray granite.

P&H TRUCK STOP

The P&H Truck Stop is ideally situated for catering to the truckin' crowd, sitting as it does just off I-91 in Wells River, a direct shot from Canada to points south. Though smaller than its sprawling Midwest truck-stop cousins, the P&H offers a full contingent of amenities for gear jammers. But it's the tasty fare of the French/English menu for which the P&H is best known: all-day breakfasts (because truckers don't operate on normal clocks), home-baked goods, plenty of comfort foods, and luscious pies galore. Night-owl college students swear by P&H pie and coffee at 3:00 a.m., and families drive for hours for Sunday brunch, after which they loosen their belts and drive back home, smiling.

The pot roast, meatloaf, and hot turkey sandwich—with hunks of real turkey—are works of art, as are the chicken-fried steak, hash browns, elk burgers, broasted chicken, poutine (fries topped with farmer's cheese and gravy), flapjacks served with real maple syrup, and mashed potatoes made with real butter. The wait staff is friendly and no-nonsense, and the coffee is strong and copiously served.

Hungry?
Wheel on in!

P&H Truck Stop:
I-91/SR-302 (exit 17), Wells River

Though the grill is open a scant sixteen hours a day, from 6:00 a.m. to 10:00 p.m., everything else is offered round the clock—including those famous P&H pies. At a modest $3.50-ish per ample wedge and with their flaky, buttery homemade crusts, these pies are not to be ignored: apple, blueberry, apricot, lemon meringue, coconut cream, custard, raspberry, mince, strawberry rhubarb, pumpkin, cherry, chocolate cream, Reese's, pecan, Boston cream, banana cream, Snickers, Vermont maple cream, and Mile-High Pie. If, for some odd reason, you're not a pie person, there's homemade cheesecake, strawberry short cake, carrot cake, whoopie pies, toasted maple nut bread, and more!

The home-baked bread loaves are massive, thick, and hearty. In fact, the P&H is synonymous with "big," as in big helpings, big breads, big pies, big clientele. About the only thing the P&H isn't big on is price. A hungry couple can dine well, with a tip, for twenty-five dollars. The only trouble is in deciding what to eat there and what to take home. . . . 10-4, good buddy.

FALL FOLIAGE

For a handful of weeks each autumn, beginning in early to mid-September and running right through October, Vermont is transformed from one of the world's prettiest places to the world's prettiest place. A bold statement, to be sure, but if you've ever seen Vermont's hillsides radiant in peak autumn color, you'll find it difficult to disagree.

Vermont's early Native American tribes believed that the Great Bear was slain daily by a hunter in the sky and that the bear's blood dripping down to earth is what colors the leaves red. Science's explanation is a complicated process involving cool nights, waning daylight, dwindling chlorophyll, and the emergence of glucose stored in the leaves. What it all adds up to, slain beast or science, is a stunning show of brilliant color unmatched anywhere.

Peak color (a misnomer, as it's a season-long evolution) happens at different times throughout the state, though the average fullest color appears, north to south, from late September through mid October. Vermont's sugar, black,

In autumn, Vermont is the prettiest place on earth: www.vermontvacation.com

and yellow maples share the hillsides with ash, birch, poplar, and oak trees, all of which offer their own particular shades to this statewide palette of beauty, though none are as brilliant as the maples, whose glucose levels produce the most visually arresting reds, stunning purples, and glowing golds.

There are as many ways to peep the leaves as there are people who yearn to see them. In Vermont, you can admire autumn's glory from the air via planes and hot-air balloons; from a lake, pond, or river, where the reflection of the trees in the water's glassy surface doubles the pleasure; from atop mountains with 360-degree views, including via Jay Peak's Aerial Tram ride or Stowe's Gondola Skyride; or from driving along thousands of miles of back roads beneath canopies of arching old-growth maples.

Visitors to Vermont should be forewarned, though: Planning ahead is a good idea. Fall is a busy season, and hotels, motels, B&Bs, and inns book up well in advance. And for good reason: It's the prettiest show on earth.

SNOWFLAKE BENTLEY

We've all heard the phrase: "No two snowflakes are alike." It was a humble Vermont farmer who first posited the theory. Born in Jericho, Vermont, on February 9, 1865, Wilson Alwyn "Snowflake" Bentley was a winter baby who never lost his zeal for the colder months. From an early age, Wilson exhibited a fascination with snow crystals (the proper name of snowflakes). When he was fifteen, he began using an old microscope given to him by his doting mother to study what he called "ice flowers" and "tiny miracles of beauty."

On January 15, 1885, during a snowstorm, young Bentley captured the first photomicrographs of snow crystals—after years of hard work, failed attempts, and disapproval from his father. He would go on to make more than five thousand such images in his lifetime with his specially devised bellows camera-microscope.

Bentley labored alone at his task for more than a dozen years, perfecting his techniques. Because his work required cold temperatures, he spent hours outdoors making his stunning images. Eventually, a University of Vermont

See what this Vermont farmer was so passionate about: www.snowflakebentley.com

professor convinced him to share his work, leading to a string of well-received articles in *Monthly Weather Review, National Geographic, Popular Scientific Monthly, Scientific American, Nature,* and many other publications.

This self-taught man of science, considered odd by his fellow Jericho natives, passed away—in the winter, naturally, and of pneumonia—on December 23, 1931 . . . a few weeks after the publication of his book, *Snow Crystals,* which contained 2,500 of his photographs. The Jericho Historical Society has established a fine Snowflake Bentley website and the Bentley Museum, a permanent exhibit at the Old Red Mill in Jericho.

Despite the technical limitations imposed by the equipment he used, many of the techniques Wilson A. Bentley developed are still in use today. The camera he used to capture images of his last snow crystal (number 5,381) was the same camera he'd used forty-five years earlier to capture his first. Snowflake Bentley's stark, white-on-black snow crystal images still have the power to startle the viewer with their pure grace. Tiny miracles of beauty, indeed.

BURLINGTON

Regularly voted as one of the most livable places in America, Burlington attracts folks from all walks of life, including nudists, artists, students, beer makers, sailors, shoppers, celebrities, artisans, high-tech manufacturers, scientists, farmers . . . you name it. Everyone who visits falls in love with Vermont's Queen City, located along scenic Lake Champlain.

In 2008, the US Centers for Disease Control and Prevention named Burlington the healthiest metropolitan area in the country, with the largest proportion of healthy folks: a whopping 92 percent! In 2009, *Children's Health Magazine* rated Burlington as the best city in the country for raising a family.

The first whites to settle in the area came in 1763. Today, Burlington is the shire town of Chittenden County and Vermont's largest city, with a head count of roughly 210,000, close to one-third of the state's population. One of the biggest feathers in the city's cap, the University of Vermont, was founded in 1791 by Green Mountain Boy, Ira Allen, and is one of the oldest colleges in the United States. The city is also home to Burlington College and Champlain College.

Vermont's Queen City is open for business— and fun! www.ci.burlington .vt.us

More than a place to hit the books, Burlington is home to a vibrant nightlife, fine dining, and numerous arts and cultural events that punctuate every month of the calendar. Crowd favorites are the Vermont Brewers' Festival and the Discover Jazz Festival, held each June at the Flynn Center for the Performing Arts.

The heart of Burlington's downtown is its famous cobbled pedestrian mall, Church Street Marketplace. This historic district comes alive with vendors, musicians, and strolling shoppers and offers boutiques and restaurants surrounded by historic architecture. The stunning waterfront of this lakeside city can be enjoyed by all from Battery Park. Burlington sports its own International Airport, and a ferry travels from Burlington to New York.

Burlington is the birthplace of numerous innovations (Ben & Jerry's!) and such notable folks as the band Phish, formed by UVM students in 1983, and Horatio Nelson Jackson, who, along with a friend, in 1903, became the first person to drive an automobile across the United States. The car was named *The Vermont*.

DANFORTH PEWTER

Few folks nowadays can claim that their life's work is in their blood. But Fred Danforth can—six generations' worth. A climb up the Danforth family tree reveals nearly two dozen pewtersmiths tucked among its branches. So many, in fact, that Fred Danforth can claim a direct lineage to his great great great great great grandfather, pewtersmith Thomas Danforth I, who plied his trade between 1733 and 1786. It was his son, Thomas Danforth II, who pioneered pewtermaking in the United States (Connecticut) between 1755 and 1782 . . . and also found time to beget seven offspring, six of them future pewterers. Busy man.

Since pewter was the tableware of choice for discerning eighteenth- and nineteenth-century Americans, the Danforths specialized in such much-needed items as plates, mugs, bowls, candlesticks, flagons, and teapots. Some of those early pieces bearing the Danforth mark can be found in collections at Colonial Williamsburg, the Smithsonian, and the Museum of Fine Arts in Boston.

In 1975, Fred Danforth and his wife, Judi, revived the dormant family

Visitors are most welcome at Danforth Pewter 52 Seymour Street, Middlebury www.danforth pewter.com

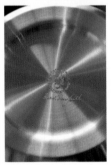

art and founded Danforth Pewterers. They began in Woodstock, and in 1988, moved their workshop to Middlebury, where all world-famous Danforth pewter is handmade today.

Pewter is an alloy composed of the metals tin, copper, and antimony. Danforth's pewter is the top of line: 100 percent lead-free fine pewter that meets or exceeds all FDA food-safety standards. It also will not tarnish, is easily cared for, and will develop its own warm patina with use.

A visit to Danforth Pewter's home workshop and store in Middlebury (they also have retail shops in Burlington, Quechee, and Waterbury) reveals a gallery of unique works as well as a collection of antique Danforth pieces. Visitors can peek through windows into the workshop, where Fred's innate artistry is revealed as he makes one-of-a-kind pewter oil lamps on antique lathes. In a nearby studio Judi designs cast items, such as jewelry, ornaments, baby items, and kitchenware. As the Danforth logo states: "fine handcrafted pewter." With hundreds of years of experience behind them, how could they miss?

WOODPILES

Woodpiles are everywhere in Vermont. Frequently handsome things, they appear in a variety of shapes and sizes: square-ended straight rows, artfully heaped into dome-topped beehive shapes, or just plain dumped in ignoble piles. Some folks line their property with chest-high rows of split and stacked firewood, forming a useful barricade that can end up a semi-permanent fixture of the yard—depending on the duration of the winter.

If they don't have a woodshed, most woodburners tarp their stacks to keep the weather off, because wet wood means weak, hissing fires. A good, dry woodpile represents insurance against the bone-chilling cold that comes with winter in the Green Mountain State, where temperatures can dip to a frigid twenty, thirty, or even forty degrees below zero.

No heat is as pervasive and comforting as that generated by a nice, slow-burning chunk of hardwood. The most common types of firewood available in Vermont are beech, maple, birch, ash, and cherry. It's available as green wood, seasoned (a year old), or seasoned and dry (the premium stuff). Kiln-dried

Cut, split, stack, haul to house, load stove, burn, empty ashes, repeat . . .

wood offers even more heat per piece, as the moisture content is so low.

A cord of seasoned wood, cut, split, and delivered, costs roughly $225 and should measure four feet high, four feet wide, and eight feet long when stacked tight. Some folks buy it log length and render it into usable hunks themselves, a formidable but satisfying chore. It has been said that firewood heats you more than once: When you cut it, when you split it, when you stack it, and finally, when you burn it—to say nothing of the joules (units of heat) generated in hauling it in from the woodpile and kindling a fire in the woodstove.

Speaking of which, Vermont is home to Vermont Castings, maker of handsome, world-famous woodstoves for more than thirty-five years. And Carts Vermont manufactures the popular Woodchuck Log Hauler.

While it's still technically burning wood, the recent popularity of wood pellets as a fuel source is a little troubling: Surely, there's more fun and hearty exercise to be had in lugging armloads of tangy-smelling firewood. Besides, those little pellets don't stack worth a bean.

LAKE CHAMPLAIN

Lake Champlain, named after French explorer Samuel de Champlain after he "discovered" it in 1609, is an international body of water with a surface area of 490 square miles. It spans the US–Canada border and is bookended on the west by New York's Adirondacks and on the east by Vermont's Greens. It's 121 miles long, fourteen miles wide at its widest point, and averages sixty-four feet deep, though it does plunge to four hundred feet in one spot. The lake is also home to eighty islands, numerous birds, myriad fish, and at least one suspected plesiosaur—aka lake monster—known as Champ.

For a brief period in 1998, Champlain became the official sixth Great Lake, from March 6 to March 24, when President Clinton signed a bill authorizing it as such, but numerous complaints made it a short-lived designation. Ice fishermen, duck hunters, fishermen, and yachters, both sail and motor, all share proprietary feelings about "their" Champlain, a watery paradise that even offers access, via canals, to the Hudson River and on to the Atlantic Ocean. At one time, Champlain sported six

Vermont's greatest lake!

Lake Aquarium and Science Center: www.echo vermont.org

Lake Champlain Maritime Museum: www.lcmm.org

Lake Champlain Chocolates: www.lake champlain chocolates.com

manned lighthouses, and it has become a popular spot for divers to explore many of her three hundred recorded historic shipwrecks. Some of the wrecks are part of the Lake Champlain Underwater Historic Preserve System. The lake also has a colorful history of smuggling, especially during Prohibition.

The Echo Lake Aquarium and Science Center and the Leahy Center for Lake Champlain, in Burlington, is an impressive complex offering visitors the chance to see a variety of the lake's fish species, including the prehistoric-looking sturgeon, in a seven-thousand-gallon aquarium. And award-winning Lake Champlain Chocolates employs one hundred people who produce more than one million pounds of gourmet chocolates each year.

The strangest Lake Champlain-related happening is the Giant Pumpkin Regatta, an annual event in which teams race in massive (one thousand pounds and up) hollowed-out pumpkins, paddling furiously in the naturally buoyant melons. No word yet on whether Champ likes the taste of pumpkin.

COUNTRY INNS

As industrialization crept into southern New England in the early nineteenth century, trains from Boston, Providence, and New York carried the well-heeled northward to discover the ample hidden charms of Vermont's hills and dales. Once there, they demanded fine accommodation.

Vermont's inns are rooted in that grand tradition, but now such longtime amenities as historic rooms filled with antiques (four-poster beds!), delectable breakfasts, tasty teas, blazing fireplaces, and tranquil settings are augmented with such offerings as day spas, riding packages, and wine-and-food-themed weekends. But it is the home-away-from-home accommodations and the knowledgeable innkeepers that turn new visitors into return guests.

There is certainly no shortage of cozy, fascinating country inns to experience throughout the state. Built in 1764, the Walloomsac Inn in Bennington is Vermont's oldest inn, while the Dorset Inn on the Green is the state's oldest continually operating inn, providing fine accommodations and dining for more than two hundred years. The Old Tavern

Vermont
is weekend
getaway central!

www.vermont
vacation.com

www.vtinns.com

at Grafton, in operation since 1801, is one of America's oldest operating inns.

The Inn at Shelburne Farms is sited in the midst of 1,400 acres of a working historic farm. The Woodstock Inn & Resort offers 142 rooms in a classic setting. The Inn at Round Barn Farm, Waitsfield, sits amidst a country landscape. The Battenkill Inn, 1840s, sits on the banks of the famed Battenkill River. The Waybury Inn in East Middlebury was pictured in the TV show *Newhart,* and Waterbury's Old Stagecoach Inn dates from 1824.

Built in 1801, the Buckmaster Inn in Shrewsbury is listed on the National Register of Historic Places, as is Rowell's Inn in Andover. The Village Country Inn in Manchester sports a one-hundred-foot porch. The Inn at Mountain View Farm in Burke sits on a historic, 440-acre farm, while in nearby Lyndonville, the historic Wildflower Inn sits on 570 acres.

Then there's Willoughvale Inn in Westmore, Rabbit Hill Inn in Lower Waterford, and, of course, Brandon Inn and Quechee Inn. . . . It's never too early to plan a weekend getaway—or three.

THE NORTHEAST KINGDOM

In a 1949 speech, US Senator and former Vermont Governor George D. Aiken extolled the singular virtues of the three counties that made up the northeast corner of his beloved state—Essex, Orleans, and Caledonia—referring to the region as the "Northeast Kingdom." The name stuck, although today locals just call it "the Kingdom."

Famous for its weather (six-month winters and stunning summers), rolling farmlands, raw wilderness, and friendly people, the Northeast Kingdom can feel to visitors as if they've found a lost world.

The Kingdom is made up of fifty-five towns and gores, and it contains one-fifth of Vermont's land mass and 25 percent of its water (including two hundred bodies of water, twelve of which are lakes). About 80 percent of the Kingdom is forest, some of which grows up the slopes of Jay Peak Ski Area and Resort, the highest spot in the Kingdom, at 3,858 feet.

Her natural beauty is unsurpassed. Consider Willoughby Gap and Willoughby Lake, the deepest lake contained within Vermont. Architecture and history are well represented with Brownington's

How to get there: In Vermont, head northeast. If you hit Canada or New Hampshire, back up.

Old Stone House Museum, built in 1834 by Reverend Alexander Twilight, the nation's first African-American college graduate and state legislator. Derby Line's Haskell Free Library and Opera House, opened in 1904, was built to straddle the Vermont–Canada border, a region rife with Prohibition-era rum running.

Artists find the Kingdom a nurturing, inspiring place—among them, painter Theodore Robinson and writer Howard Frank Mosher. Cultural offerings include Circus Smirkus in Greensboro, Bread & Puppet Theater in Glover, and Kingdom County Productions in Barnet. Danville is home to both the Great Vermont Corn Maze and the American Society of Dowsers. And the world-class Fairbanks Museum and Planetarium resides in St. Johnsbury.

In 2006, the Northeast Kingdom was called the most desirable place to visit in the entire United States by the National Geographic Society, which also said it was the ninth most desirable place in the world. Residents of the Kingdom chuckle at this. After all, they can't think of a single place in the world any lovelier, let alone eight. . . .

ETHAN ALLEN &
THE GREEN MOUNTAIN BOYS

Every Vermont school kid has heard of Vermont's most famous historic sons, the Green Mountain Boys (even though their leader, Ethan Allen, and his brother, Ira, were born in the colony of Connecticut). More than a dozen historical markers lining Vermont's roadsides as well as numerous parks, monuments, and commercial establishments throughout the state pay tribute to them.

This homegrown militia formed in the 1760s in response to corruption and thievery arising over ownership of the wilderness immediately west of the Connecticut River, known as the New Hampshire Grants. New York and New Hampshire had squabbled over the area for years, and in 1764, King George of England awarded jurisdiction of the Grants to New York. This rendered invalid deeds bought by settlers in good faith from New Hampshire's Governor Wentworth. These wronged—and irate—grant holders met in Bennington and formed the Green Mountain Boys.

Their meeting place was later renamed the Catamount Tavern, as they had placed a stuffed catamount by the

See where the famous patriot hung his tricorn hat . . .

The Ethan Allen Homestead www.ethanallenhomestead.org

door as a fierce warning to any New Yorkers who dared to displace them. During this vigilant period, the Green Mountain Boys used heavy-handed tactics to drive usurping settlers from New York off their land.

In 1775, as the American Revolution unfolded, the Green Mountain Boys helped to seize British-held New York forts at Ticonderoga and at Crown Point on Lake Champlain. In 1777, their forces, led by Seth Warner, played a pivotal role in securing victory at the Battle of Bennington. Allen was captured by the British in 1775 and, as a prisoner, learned that the state of Vermont had declared its independence in July 1777.

Allen died on February 12, 1789, at age fifty-one. In the 1850s, his original grave marker disappeared, so in 1858, the Vermont Legislature authorized erection of a statue of the famous man standing atop a forty-two-foot pillar of Vermont granite. But only a time capsule is buried beneath his monument. The precise location of Ethan Allen's remains within Burlington's Green Mount Cemetery is unknown to this day.

GENERAL STORES

You know you're in a traditional Vermont general store and not one of those newfangled mini-marts when the wooden floors squeak as you walk the narrow aisles lined with sagging shelves that groan under the weight of a hodge-podge of goods. There's a meat counter, where the owner and his long-time cohorts howl when the Red Sox win or lose. The same batch of regulars hover near the always-burnt coffee pot, saying the same things they said the day before. But rest assured, they'll pipe down when you tell the girl at the register you need a fishing or hunting license.

The Willey's Store—or Willey's, as most locals call it—is Greensboro's thumping heart. Not only can you buy all your canning supplies there, but within its jam-packed aisles you'll find a vast assortment of Vermont-made beers and cheeses. While picking up a cart full of groceries and meats, you can also outfit yourself and your kin for hunting and fishing (from toe to pate, rod to

Yep, we got that.

**The Willey's Store
7 Breezy Avenue,
Greensboro
www.willeysvt
.com**

**F. H. Gillingham
& Sons
Elm Street,
Woodstock
www.gillinghams
.com**

gun) and buy the innards for that busted toilet, the paint to spiff the shed, denim overalls, rubber barn boots, a spare crib-bage board, and the wiring to update Aunt Ethel's cherished lamp. It seems like the only thing you can't find at Willey's is the way out, if you've gotten yourself turned around in one of its many rooms.

Then there's Willey's friendly rival, F. H. Gillingham & Sons of Woodstock, a tony little burg, which might explain the preponderance of touristy items, such as books about Vermont, T-shirts, all manner of maple goods, and a great website. In the mercantile biz since 1886, Gillingham's offers an unparal-leled assortment of Vermont specialty foods, plus toys, musi-cal instruments, wool coats, Muck boots, hunting and fish-ing supplies, beer and wine, and groceries, too.

No matter the town, the general store is the place you'll find out everything worth know-ing. You can meet everyone in town there, too, if you lean by the coffee pot long enough.

VERMONT CHEDDAR CHEESE

As the world's most popular type of cheese, cheddar is renowned for its slightly crumbly, buttery texture and wide range of flavors, from mild to extra sharp. It was long ago exported from the English village of Cheddar, where it has been made since the twelfth century. Today, Wisconsin produces more cheddar than anywhere else in the world, and New York and Oregon have something to say about it, too. But it is Vermont that produces some of the world's *best* cheddar. In fact, in 2008, *Wine Spectator* magazine found that forty of the world's finest cheeses were from New England, ten of those from Vermont.

Vermont's most popular cheddar is made by Cabot Creamery, which produces a number of varieties, most notably a twenty-four-month-old "Vintage Choice" cheddar. The almost-century-old dairy co-operative proudly claims its cheese as "The World's Best" cheddar. And while it is mighty tasty, there are plenty of other cheese makers in Vermont—forty-four to date—who are challenging that notion, many with complex, award-winning cheddars of their own.

Say cheese!

Vermont Cheese Council:
www.vtcheese
.com

Cabot Creamery:
www.cabotcheese
.com

Grafton Village Cheese:
www.grafton villagecheese .com

Shelburne Farms:
www.shelburne farms.org

Grafton Village Cheese offers a variety of handcrafted premium cheddars, and Shelburne Farms produces an assortment of stunning cheddars, including two-year and smoked varieties. And Vermont Farmstead Cheese Company offers a distinctive "Artisan" cheddar. Neighborly Farms makes bold-tasting flavored cheeses, and Blythedale Farm's camembert and brie are pure cheesy pleasure.

But Vermont cheddar still dominates the dairy section of most Vermont stores, and for a simple reason: It tastes great alone or with darn near anything—crackers, a hunk of home-made bread, melted in soup, grated on salad. It is also a particularly toothsome treat with fresh-baked apple pie, still one of the finest food pairings on earth.

Uncolored pure cheddar, or white cheddar, is also known the world over as Vermont Cheddar (because Vermonters won't tolerate their "cheddar" with a nuclear-orange glow). Much like those Vermonters, Vermont Cheddar is a pleasure to get to know—at times a little nutty, often mellow, and even a tad tongue-sharp, but quality through and through.

BAG BALM

Manufactured by Dairy Association Company, Inc., in Lyndonville, the thick, magical golden goop with the consistency of petroleum jelly is known the world over as Bag Balm (aka "the stuff in the square green tin"). Developed in 1899 by a Vermont pharmacist, the recipe was purchased by a local farmer who began marketing it. Soon enough, farmers' wives noticed that their hubbies' normally rough hands were smooth, and it became apparent that the product's charms had potential far beyond the barn.

It's an ideal ointment for diaper rash, chapped hands, cuts, burns, and chafed skin. Just ask Admiral Byrd's 1937 expedition to the North Pole (the udders of their base-camp cows needed protecting) or Charles Kuralt, who reported from *On the Road* in 1983 that 400,000 tins of Bag Balm were shipping annually (the number's increased since then). The Allied Troops in WWII (it helped protect their weapons), the dogs working at Ground Zero following the September 11, 2001, terrorist attacks in New York City (it protected and soothed their paws), and US troops

It's in the can!

www.bagbalm .com

in Afghanistan and Iraq have received tins of Bag Balm in care packages. Its wonders have also been extolled on the *Oprah Winfrey Show* and in *Glamour* magazine, the *New York Times, Bicycling Magazine,* and *USA Today.* Bag Balm isn't just for Ol' Bossy anymore.

Today, it's as probable you'll see stacks of the familiar can in boutique shops in the Big Apple as on the shelf of a small-town Vermont feed shop. Available in three sizes, including the 4.5-pound plastic tub (preferred by farmers), the ten-ounce can (popular with families), and the demure one-ounce can (perfect for the purse). Whatever its size, each green tin is visually arresting (and useful when empty), and bears the slogan, "It's like having another hand on the farm or a helper around the house."

Dairy Association Company also offers two other popular products: TackMaster, for leather care, and Green Mountain Hoof Softener, for damaged hooves. But it is the perennial popularity of its flagship stalwart, Bag Balm, that buoys the company boat and ensures it will float for a long time to come.

BENNINGTON BATTLE DAY

Despite the fact that the Battle of Bennington Day is an official Vermont state holiday, the battle itself, which occurred on August 16, 1777, actually took place ten miles to the west, near Walloomsac Heights . . . in New York. But never mind such piffling details, because Vermont has the 306-foot-tall Bennington Battle Monument, and New York doesn't.

On the morning of the battle, General Stark reportedly said to his men, "There are your enemies, the Red Coats and the Tories. They are ours, or this night Molly Stark sleeps a widow." Despite this rousing guilt trip—er, pep talk—if on that day General Stark and Colonel Seth Warner and his Green Mountain Boys hadn't defeated British General John Burgoyne's men, Burgoyne may well have won his next engagement, at Saratoga, instead of surrendering. But Stark's men managed to reduce the enemy by one thousand, depriving them of the desperately needed weapons, munitions, animals, and other supplies they had intended to steal from the depot at Bennington.

Bennington celebrates Battle Day over several days revolving around

Bennington Battle Monument: 15 Monument Circle, Bennington www.bennington.com

August 16, with a parade, Revolutionary War reenactments, and numerous other festivities. Most of the events take place at Bennington Battle Monument, erected where those much sought-after supplies were stored more than two centuries ago.

The monument, completed in 1889, is the tallest man-made structure in Vermont. Though it was supposed to be 100 feet tall, the final design ended up at 306 feet. Composed of New York dolomite, the statue took two years to build and cost $112,000. It was dedicated in 1891 by President Benjamin Harrison, who then enjoyed libations at the nearby Walloomsac Inn.

From the monument's internal observatory two-thirds of the way up—reached via elevator—visitors can take in stunning views of Vermont, New York, and Massachusetts. The monument grounds also house statues of General Stark, Colonel Seth Warner, and other important persons of the day.

Meanwhile, back in New York, the 1,250-acre Bennington Battlefield, a US National Historic Landmark, is open to visitors year-round.

MAPLE SYRUP

Maple syrup is so important to Vermont culturally, economically, and socially that a nostalgic maple sap collection scene is featured on the Vermont state quarter, the state's official tree is the sugar maple, and the state's official flavor is . . . maple. That's because Vermont is the largest US producer of the lip-smacking sweet stuff, generating 5.5 percent of the entire world's supply—1.14 million gallons in 2011.

From mid-February into April, roughly a six-week stretch when days begin to warm and nights are still long and cold, starches stored in trees convert to sugars and rise up the trunks. Long before white European settlers arrived in North America, indigenous peoples tapped trees for the sweet spring sap the Algonquin called sinzibuckwud, which translates as "drawn from trees." Over the following centuries, more efficient gathering methods were devised.

Today, most commercial syrup makers use plastic pipeline strung from tree to tree. A stand of tapped trees can include sugar, black, red, and silver maples. The stand is called a "sugarbush," the building to which all that sap

How sweet it is!

St. Albans Maple Festival: www.vtmaple festival.org

Vermont Maple Foundation: www.vermont maple.org

is ferried for processing is called a "sugarhouse," and boiling down the sap to make syrup is called "sugaring." It takes forty gallons of sap to make one gallon of syrup, and the dry, sweet steam of sap slowly evaporating in a sugarhouse is a heady perfume like no other.

Maple syrup is categorized by its density, flavor, and color, and comes in fancy, medium amber, dark amber, and grade B categories, with varying degrees of favor intensity. It is a healthful product low in sodium and rich in antioxidants, but it's the flavor that keeps people hooked, especially in maple cream, maple fudge, maple jelly, maple salad dressing, maple mustard, maple butter, maple cotton candy, maple ice cream. . . .

Many Vermonters are sweet on a delicacy called "sugar on snow"—maple syrup drizzled on snow, then rolled on a fork, and often accompanied with a dill pickle! You, too, can indulge in this treat at the Vermont Maple Open House Weekend, held every April, an event only outdone by the St. Albans Vermont Maple Festival, a three-day affair that attracts 50,000 maple maniacs.

STOWE

Though granted a charter in 1763, Stowe remained unsettled until 1793, when Oliver Luce and his family made the trek on foot in winter. (The sled they dragged is on display at the Stowe Historical Society's Museum on Main Street.) By the mid-nineteenth century, it had become the largest township in the state, with farming, lumbering, and maple sugaring forming a large part of its industry.

The state's first official ski trails were carved on Stowe's Mt. Mansfield, Vermont's highest spot at 4,395 feet, by 1933. Today, Stowe is home to the forty-eight-trail Stowe Mountain Resort, a world-class, year-round destination. Stoweflake Mountain Resort and Spa and the Topnotch Resort and Spa are also in Stowe, and close by is Smugglers' Notch (aka Smuggs).

In 1941, the famous von Trapp Family Singers (inspiration for *The Sound of Music* musical and film) settled in Stowe, and in the 1950s they opened a rustic chalet-style lodge for winter adventurers. After a fire destroyed the chalet in 1980, the family rebuilt in grand fashion, in 1983 opening the world-famous Trapp Family Lodge, a ninety-six-room, four-star resort and ski-touring center.

Stowe Chamber of Commerce: www.gostowe.com

Trapp Family Lodge: www.trappfamily.com

Stowe Mountain Resort: www.stowe.com

The tony town of Stowe manages to offer the top-shelf amenities that well-heeled vacationers expect while retaining its small-town charm. Visitors are never far from outdoor adventure (in 1981, Stowe constructed its 5.3-mile Recreation Path, a paved exercise trail open year-round) or from more leisurely pursuits such as shopping, spa treatments, and fine dining. Stowe claims to be surpassed only by Boston and Providence when it comes to award-winning New England eateries—and one of Stowe's best is Cliff House Restaurant, near the top of Mt. Mansfield.

Every September since 1991, Stowe hosts the British Invasion, the largest British Automobile Show and celebration in New England. Since 1986, Stoweflake Mountain Resort and Spa has held its annual Hot Air Balloon Festival in July, proving that, even though winter sports put Stowe on the tourist map, it's the resort town's charm and diverse offerings that keep it thriving year-round.

DEER CAMP

Hunters in Vermont harvest nearly one million pounds of venison each year, among them more bucks per square mile than in any other New England state. Impressive, to be sure, but deer season is really all about the heady, nostril-twitching aroma of sopping wool socks draped over a chair by the cast-iron woodstove, bright orange hats, and red-and-black-check jackets steaming on their pegs on the wall.

As much a Vermont tradition as is sugaring season, attending deer camp (aka "goin' up to camp") is a holdover from a time when men trekked deep into the back country to hunt, making do in rough little shelters while they went about the business of providing for their families. Nowadays, deer camps don't have to be all that far from home, and they are decidedly less austere affairs. Some sport running water, electricity, and an indoor privy, and most offer a hodgepodge of cast-off furnishings from attendees' homes.

The prevailing sentiment among camp visitors is one of modest privation,

See you "up to camp". . .

www.vtfishand wildlife.com

if only for a few cherished days spent reconnecting with a core group of friends and family. A typical deer camp day begins with a hearty breakfast before sunup and is followed by daylight hours of hunting interrupted with a midday reconnoiter at camp for a hot meal. Later on, a few hands of penny poker and a tumbler of The Famous Grouse help round out the evening.

There's no way of knowing how many deer camps are in Vermont, but if you happen to wander the Green Mountains and come upon a moss-sided shanty with a rusty stovepipe leaning slightly askew, you may have found someone's little slice of heaven. The man who inherited it will most likely pass it on to his son or daughter, and so on. And it will continue to be a gathering place for friends and family to share time-honored rituals, stories, and values, passing them from one generation to the next, creating memories and continuing traditions.

Oh, and that vinyl, mustard-colored swivel chair from Uncle Larry's rec room? Perfect for camp.

VERMONT COMMON CRACKERS

Is there anything more bucolic than that timeworn vision of checker-playing cronies gathered 'round the mercantile's potbelly stove on a winter afternoon, cussing their poor moves and absent-mindedly reaching into the brimming cracker barrel for a snack? Ever wonder where those old-time crackers came from?

In 1828, the Cross Brothers of Montpelier decided to start a commercial bakery focusing on crackers. Those early efforts were made three days a week on a contraption powered by a horse on a treadmill that the enterprising brothers built themselves. On the days when they weren't making crackers, the brothers peddled their goods in barrels and sacks to homes, businesses, and to the train station for delivery to farther locales.

Aside from a few subsequent owners, a name change, and a couple of tweaks to the recipe, those "Montpelier Crackers" are still being made today, nine generations of satisfied Vermonters later. Nowadays, though, they're called Vermont Common Crackers, and the new owners, the Orton Family, are proprietors of the world-famous Vermont Country Store.

Got soup (but no crackers)?

Vermont Common Foods: www.vermont commonfoods .com

The Vermont Country Store: Weston & Rockingham www.vermont countrystore.com

Although the sound of hoofbeats in the factory is but a memory today, a dedicated crew oversees the entire Common Cracker manufacturing process, making two flavors: traditional and cheddar (with award-winning Grafton Village Vermont Cheddar, naturally). The crackers are available in two sizes, regular and bite-size, and in a 7.5-ounce box or a 16-ounce tin. While Vermont Common Crackers are ideal with cheese, jam, or any combination of appetizer, most folks float them on their chowder, soups or stews, or better yet, crumble them into a bowl of milk, just like old-time Vermonters.

The Orton family's Vermont Common Crackers have gained long and steady high praise, with appearances on *The Rachael Ray Show* and the *Today Show* as well as in the *Boston Globe* and *Martha Stewart Living* magazine.

As popular as they were 183-plus years ago when they were first introduced by Montpelier's Cross brothers, Vermont Common Crackers can be found most anywhere crackers are sold. Or wherever there's a Vermonter with a bowl of milk and a checkerboard.

SNOW

In the fall, the ubiquitous woolly worm—that fuzzy, black-ended caterpillar with the brown band in the middle—is a prognosticator of how long a winter the frozen north can expect. A wide band of brown means we're in for a long, snowy winter. Never fails. . . . Snowbirds see this and fly south— a common affliction that affects a goodly number of Vermonters (native and non), especially in their golden years.

Early storms, sometimes in mid- to late-October, can dump a foot or two of snow, letting the weak know that it's time to pack up and the old hands that it's time to put on the stewpot, stoke the stove, and fire up the snowmobile. Every few years, Vermont gets hammered by a record breaker, such as the big Valentine's Day storm of 2007 that dumped forty-eight inches on Stowe. The state regularly hosts Nor'easters—storms that descend like rogue locomotives from the northeast, bringing forty to fifty inches of snow and six foot drifts. Ski areas love winter in Vermont.

From November through April, Vermont is a white wonderland. www.vermont vacation.com

Studded tires for cars and chains for big trucks are common, as are extra layers of clothes. For months on end, the only green to be seen is on the little screen in the living room, showing a golf tournament somewhere far south.

Too many people don't know what they're missing, though, hibernating in their plastic-wrapped homes, chucking firewood into the stove, and hoping to see a drip from the eaves. Winter in the Green Mountain State can be a whole lot of fun: Snowmobiling is an official Vermont obsession, enabled by 4,500 miles of trails statewide winding through otherwise inaccessible beautiful back country. Skiing, sledding, skating, snowshoeing, hunting, building snowmen and snow forts, going on sleigh rides, attending winter festivals, and participating in ice-fishing tournaments. . . . The list of snow-centric distractions in Vermont is long and filled with fun—provided folks get out and about in it.

Vermont in the winter? Can't change it, so . . . let it snow, let it snow, let it snow!

PHOTO CREDITS

All photos © Jennifer Smith-Mayo except: p.58, © Library of Congress; p. 68, © Wilson Bentley/ National Oceanic and Atmospheric Administration (Snow Crystals); and p. 69, © Wilson Bentley.

ACKNOWLEDGMENTS

We wish to thank the following for their kind assistance during the compilation of this book: Charity Smith—for being the best photo assistant and greatest "Sistah" a sistah could have! Our parents, Rose Mary and David Smith and Gayla and Bill Mayo, for following those back roads that led you to Vermont; Jen and Jeff (Meisterbro!); Michael Hunter Smith; Guinness and Nessie; Guy; the Royer family, finest of friends; Jason and Chance; the Deer Camp Crew; the Burdick family (and Gert's mac-n-cheese!); E. M. Brown & Sons; Erin Turner; Lake Region Youth Baseball; Laurie and Bernard LaBounty; Jed's Maple; Annie Mcneil; Vermont Pub & Brewery; Vermont Brewers Festival; Brad Nutt and Zero Gravity; Rosalyn Graham and the cheesemakers and chefs at Shelburne Farms & Inn; Johnson Woolen Mills; Green Mountain Coffee; Bag Balm; Bennington

Slope Sistahs Jen Smith-Mayo (left) and Charity Smith (right).

Potters; Shelburne Museum; Vermont Teddy Bear Company; F. H. Gillingham & Sons store crew; Willey's store crew; Ben & Jerry's; Caleb Palazzo; the town of Calais; Paul Williams; Fairbanks Museum; Trapp Family Lodge; Jasmine McLean and Stowe Area Association; Jay Peak Ski Resort; LT Hikers Splake and Sponge; The Inn at Long Trail; UVM Morgan Horse Farm; Burtt's Orchard; Madeline Cushing; Mary Beth and Dick Young and crew; Sheb White; Vermont Common Cracker crew; Cold Hollow Cider Mill; Billings Farm & Museum; Craig Calamaio; Senator Bernie Sanders; Kelsey and Justin Villone; P&H Truck Stop; Rock of Ages Quarry; Jericho Historical Society; Danforth Pewter; Old Stagecoach Inn; Strong House Inn; Ethan Allen Homestead; and the living history regiments at Bennington Monument.